COGAT®
GRADE 2
NON-VERBAL

3 Practice Tests
Level 8

Savant Test Prep™

www.SavantPrep.com

Please leave a review for this book!

Thank you for purchasing this resource.

Please take a moment to leave a
review on the website where you purchased this.

TABLE OF CONTENTS

INTRODUCTION

COGAT® GENERAL INFORMATION

- COGAT® stands for Cognitive Abilities Test®.
- The test measures students' reasoning skills and problem-solving skills.
- It provides educators with an overall assessment of students' academic strengths and weaknesses.
- The COGAT® is commonly used as a screener for gifted and talented programs.
    - Gifted and Talented (G&T) selection sometimes requires a teacher recommendation as well.
- The test is usually administered in a group setting.
- A teacher (or other school associate) administers the test, reading the directions.
- Please check with your school/testing site regarding its testing procedures, as these may differ.

COGAT® LEVEL 8 FORMAT

- Students in second grade take the COGAT® Level 8.
- The Non-Verbal Battery has 50 questions.
- The test is divided into 3 main parts, each called a "Battery." Each Battery has three question types. See chart below.

VERBAL BATTERY	NON-VERBAL BATTERY	QUANTITATIVE BATTERY
Picture Analogies: 18 Questions	Figure Analogies: 18 Questions	Number Puzzles: 14 Questions
Picture Classification: 18 Questions	Figure Classification: 18 Questions	Number Series: 18 Questions
Sentence Completion: 18 Questions	Paper Folding: 14 Questions	Number Analogies: 18 Questions

- Often, schools administer one Battery per day, allowing approximately 45 minutes per Battery.
- Students have around 15 minutes to complete each question type (for example, students would have around 15 minutes to complete Picture Analogies).
- See the following pages for examples and explanations of each question type.

COGAT® SCORING

- Students receive points for correct answers. Points are not deducted for incorrect answers. (Therefore, students should at least guess versus leaving a question blank.)
- In general, schools have a "cut-off" COGAT® score, which they consider together with additional criteria, for gifted & talented acceptance. This varies by school.
- This score is usually at least 98%. (However, some schools accept scores of 95% or even 85%.)
- A score of 98% means that your child scored as well as, or better than, 98% of those in his/her testing group.
- COGAT® scores are available for the entire test and can be broken down by Battery.
- Depending on the school/program, such a "cut-off" score may only be required on one or two of the Batteries (and not on the test overall).
- It is essential to check with your school/program for their acceptance procedures.
- The COGAT® Practice Tests in this book can not yield these percentiles because they have not been given to a large enough group of students to produce an accurate comparison/calculation.

HOW TO USE THIS BOOK

1. Go over the Question Examples together with your child. These begin on the next page.

2. Do Practice Test 1 (Workbook Format)
   - Do these questions with your child, especially if this is your child's first exposure to COGAT®-prep questions. These questions have a "workbook format," meaning they are meant to be done together.
   - Do not assign a time limit.
   - Talk about what the question is asking your child to do.
   - Questions progress in difficulty. (The first few questions are quite simple.)
   - Go over the answers using the Answer Key.
   - For questions missed, go over the answers again, discussing what makes the correct answer better than the other choices.

3. Do the remaining Practice Tests following Practice Test 1.
   - If your child progressed easily through Practice Test 1, see how well they can do without your help.
   - If your child needed assistance with much of Practice Test 1, then continue to assist your child with Practice Test 2.
   - If you wish to assign a time limit, assign around 15 minutes per question type.
   - Go over the answers using the Answer Key.
   - For questions missed, go over the answers again, discussing what makes the correct answer better than the other choices.

4. Need more practice?

   - **Help your child ace the test!**

   - **Check out Savant Test Prep™ books on Amazon®.**

TEST-TAKING TIPS

- Ensure your child listens carefully to the directions, especially in the Sentence Completion section.
- Make sure (s)he does not rush through questions. (There is no prize for finishing first!) Tell your child to look carefully at the question. Then, tell your child to look at each answer choice before marking his/her answer.
  - If you notice your child continuing to rush through the questions, tell him/her to point to each part of the question. Then, point to each answer choice.
- If (s)he does not know the answer, then use the process of elimination. Cross out any answer choices which are clearly incorrect, then choose from those remaining.
- This tip/suggestion is entirely at your discretion. You may wish to offer some sort of special motivation to encourage your child to do his/her best. An extra incentive of, for example, an art set, a building block set, or a special outing can go a long way in motivating young learners!
- The night before testing, make sure your child has enough sleep, without any interruptions. (Think about the difference in your brain function with a good night's sleep vs. without. The same goes for your child's.)
- The morning before the test, ensure your child eats a healthy breakfast with protein and complex carbs. Do not let them eat sugar, chocolate, etc.
- If you can choose the time your child will take the test (for example, if (s)he will take the test individually, instead of at school with a group), opt for a morning testing session, when your child will be most alert.

QUESTION EXAMPLES

- Here is an overview of the COGAT® question types.
- This section has <u>simple</u> examples, to introduce your child to test concepts.
    - Do these examples together with your child.
- Below the questions are explanations for parents.

1. FIGURE ANALOGIES (NON-VERBAL BATTERY)

• **Directions (read to child):** The pictures in the top boxes go together in some way. Look at the bottom boxes. One box is empty. Look at the row of pictures next to the boxes. These are the answer choices. Which one of these choices goes with the picture in the bottom box like the pictures in the top box go together?

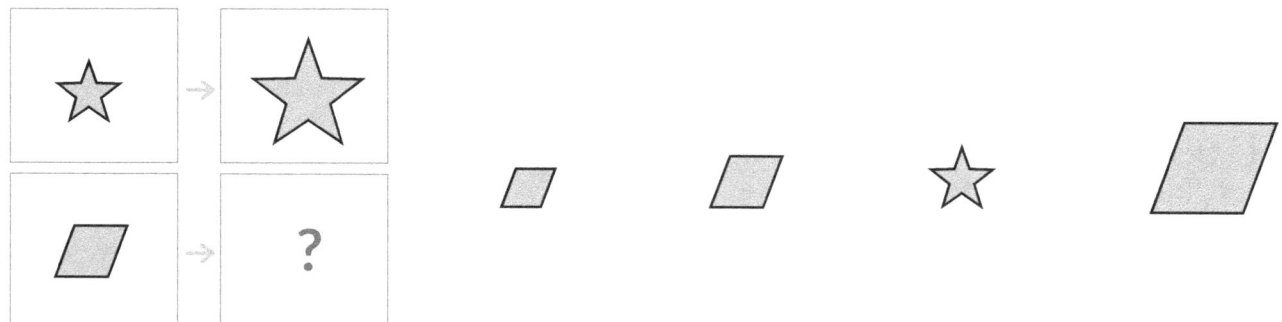

• **Using this question as an example, say to your child:** In the top left box, we see 1 star. In the top right box, we also see a star, but it has gotten bigger. Let's come up with a rule to describe how the picture has changed from left to right. From left to right, the shape gets bigger. On the bottom is a parallelogram. Let's look at the answer choices and see if any fit our rule. The first choice does not - the shape is smaller. The second choice does not - the shape is the same size. The third choice does not - it is a different shape. The last choice does - it is the same shape as the bottom box, but it is bigger.

• **Explanation (for parents):** In the directions, the word "picture" means a "figure" consisting of one or more shapes/lines/etc.

Your child must figure out how the images in top set of boxes are related and belong together. Then, (s)he must figure out which answer choice would go with the bottom left image so that the bottom set would have the same analogous relationship as the top set. (The small arrows demonstrate that the images go together.)

Try to define a "rule" to describe how the top set belongs together.

Make your "rule" describe a "change" that occurs from the top left box to the top right box.

Next, take this "rule" describing the change, and apply it to the bottom picture.

Then, look at the answer choices to determine which one would make the bottom set also follow your "rule."

If more than one answer choice fits the rule, then the rule needs to be more specific.

- The images below outline "changes" in Figure Analogy questions (how the figures change in the analogy).

- In basic Figure Analogy questions, like the example, there is one "change" -or- a change that is quite obvious.

- In the below images #1-9, there is one change.

- More advanced questions, like #10-12 below, have two changes (or changes that are not as obvious).

Directions for the below images:
- See if your child can figure out how the first picture "changes" to the second picture below.
- The questions' "change" (the logic) is at the bottom of the page.

1. 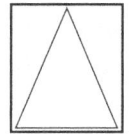 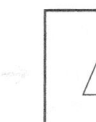 2. 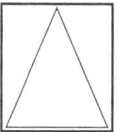 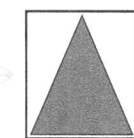 3.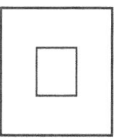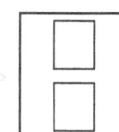

4.  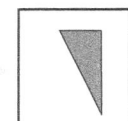 5. 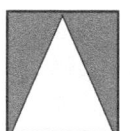 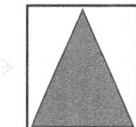 6.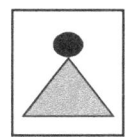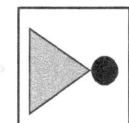

7.  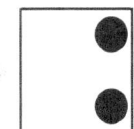 8. 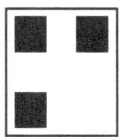 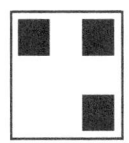 9.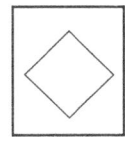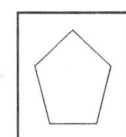

10. 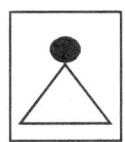 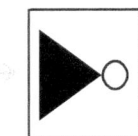 11.   12.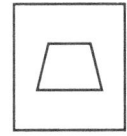

1. Size (gets smaller)
2. Color (white to dark gray)
3. Quantity (plus 1)
4. Whole to Half
5. Color Reversal
6. Rotation (clockwise, 90°)

7. Rotation (clockwise, 90°)
8. Rotation -or- Mirror Image/"Flip"
9. Number of Shape Sides (shape with +1 side)
10. Two Changes: Rotation (clockwise, 90°)
    and Color Reversal
11. Two Changes: Shape Position and Size
12. Two Changes: Shape Size and Color

2. FIGURE CLASSIFICATION (NON-VERBAL BATTERY)

• **Directions (read to child):** The top row shows three pictures that are alike in some way. Look at the bottom row. There are four pictures. Which picture in the bottom row goes best with the pictures in the top row?

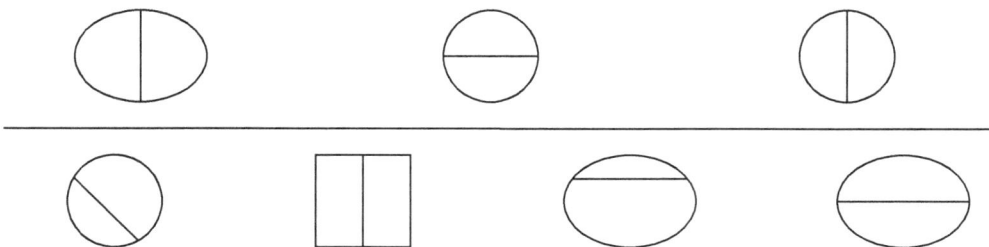

• **Explanation (for parents):** Together with your child, try to figure out a "rule" describing how the top pictures are alike and belong together. Then, apply the "rule" to each answer choice to determine which one follows it. If your child finds that more than one choice follows the rule, then a more specific rule is needed.

• **Using the above question as an example, say to your child:** Here we see 1 oval divided in half, 1 circle divided in half, and 1 circle divided in half. What is a rule that describes how they are alike? They are all round and divided in half. In the bottom row, which choice follows this rule? Choice 1 and 3 are round and divided, but not divided in half. Choice 2 is divided in half, but it is not round. Choice 4 is round and divided in half.

• The following examples include basic logic used in Figure Classification questions, with answers at the end.

• **Directions (read to child):** The top row shows three pictures that are alike in some way. Look at the bottom row. There are four pictures. Which picture in the bottom row goes best with the pictures in the top row?

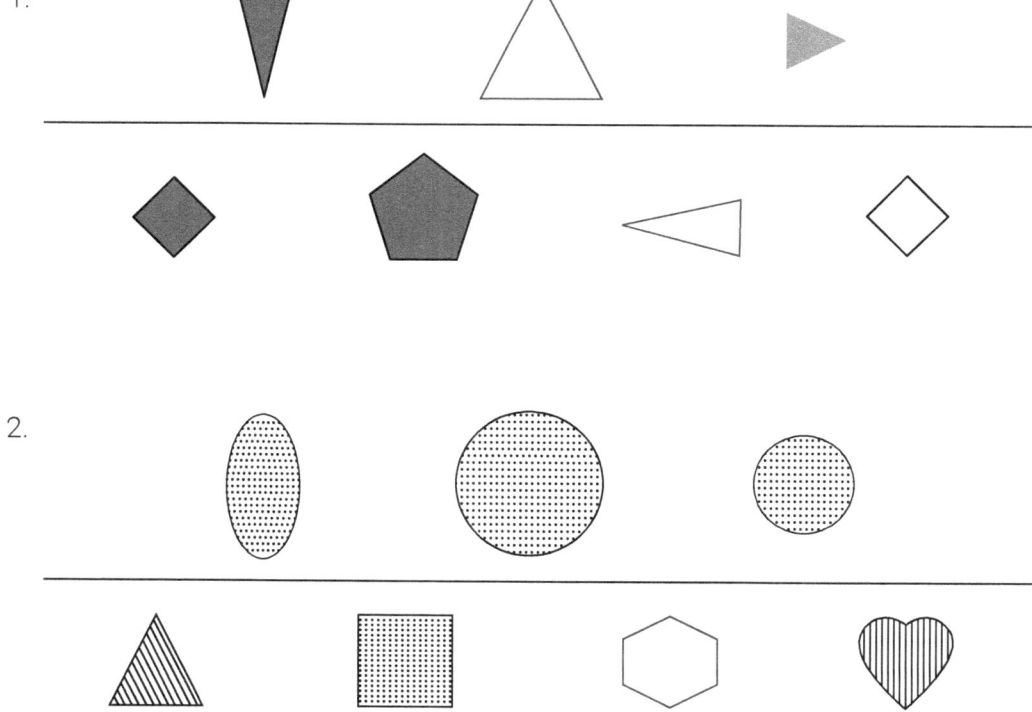

• **Note:** These are <u>more challenging</u>. If your child needs help, ask them the question next to the number.

3. Which way is it pointing?

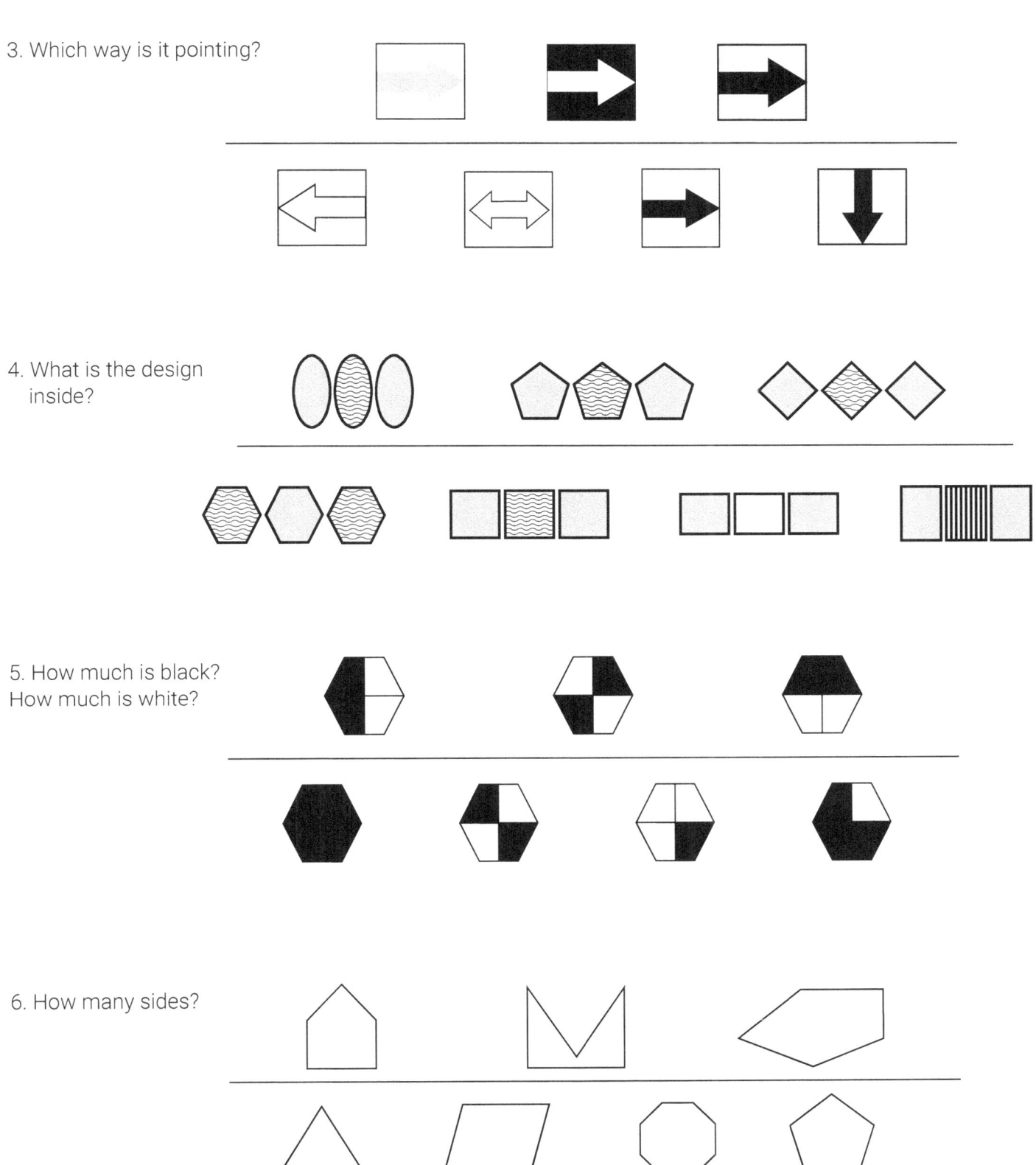

4. What is the design inside?

5. How much is black? How much is white?

6. How many sides?

1- Choice 3: triangles   2- Choice 2: filled with dots   3- Choice 3: arrows point right
4- Choice 2: the designs are gray, wavy lines, gray   5- Choice 2: half is white, half is black
6- Choice 4: the shapes have 5 sides

7. How many shapes of each kind are together next to each other?

 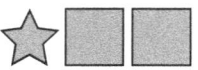 

   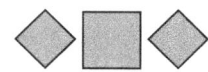

8. What kind of small shapes are there?

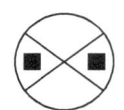  

9. What kinds of shape are gray or white? How many?

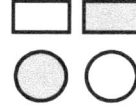  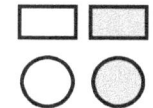

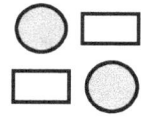 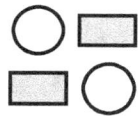 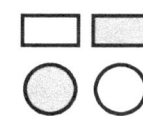 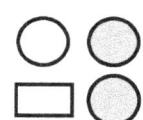

10. How many shapes are in each group?

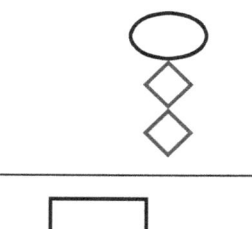 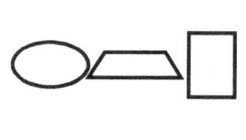 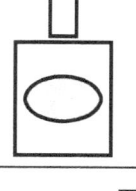

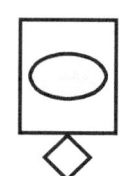  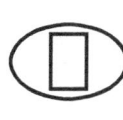 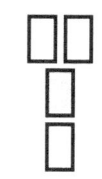

7-Choice 3: there are 2 identical shapes next to a shape that's a different kind of shape
8-Choice 4: the 2 small black shapes are the same
9-Choice 3: the 2 gray shapes are 1 rectangle and 1 circle   10-Choice 1: there are 3 shapes in the group

10

3. PAPER FOLDING (NON-VERBAL BATTERY)

• **Directions (read to child):** The top row of pictures shows a sheet of paper. The paper was folded, then something was cut out. Which picture in the bottom row shows how the paper would look after it's unfolded?

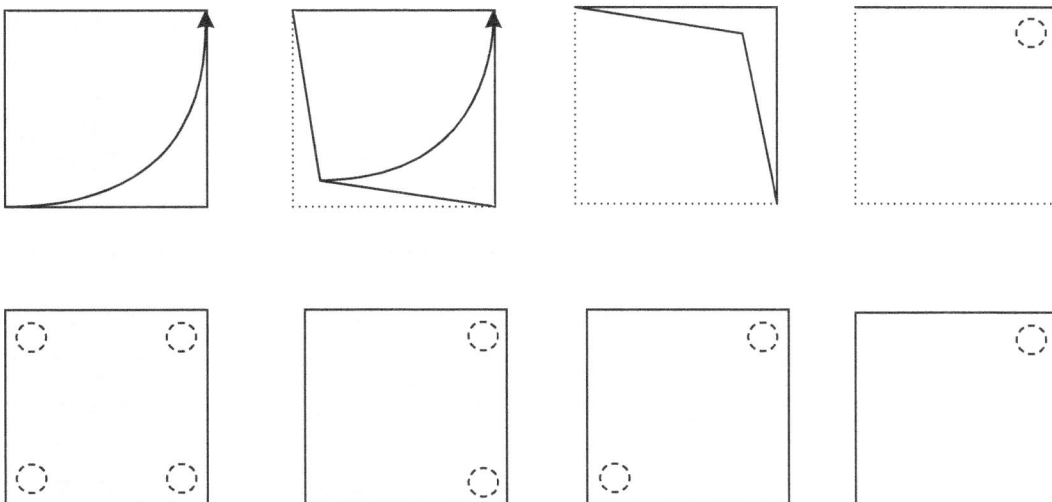

• **Explanation (read to child):** The first choice has too many holes. In the second choice, the holes are not in the correct position. The third choice has the correct number of holes and in the correct position. The last choice only shows the hole on top.

• **Tip:** If Paper Folding is challenging for your child, demonstrate using real paper and scissors. (It is common for kids to initially struggle with Paper Folding. It is not an activity most children have much experience with.)

• Show your child the following examples. Demonstrate using real paper, if needed.

Paper Folding Steps   Result

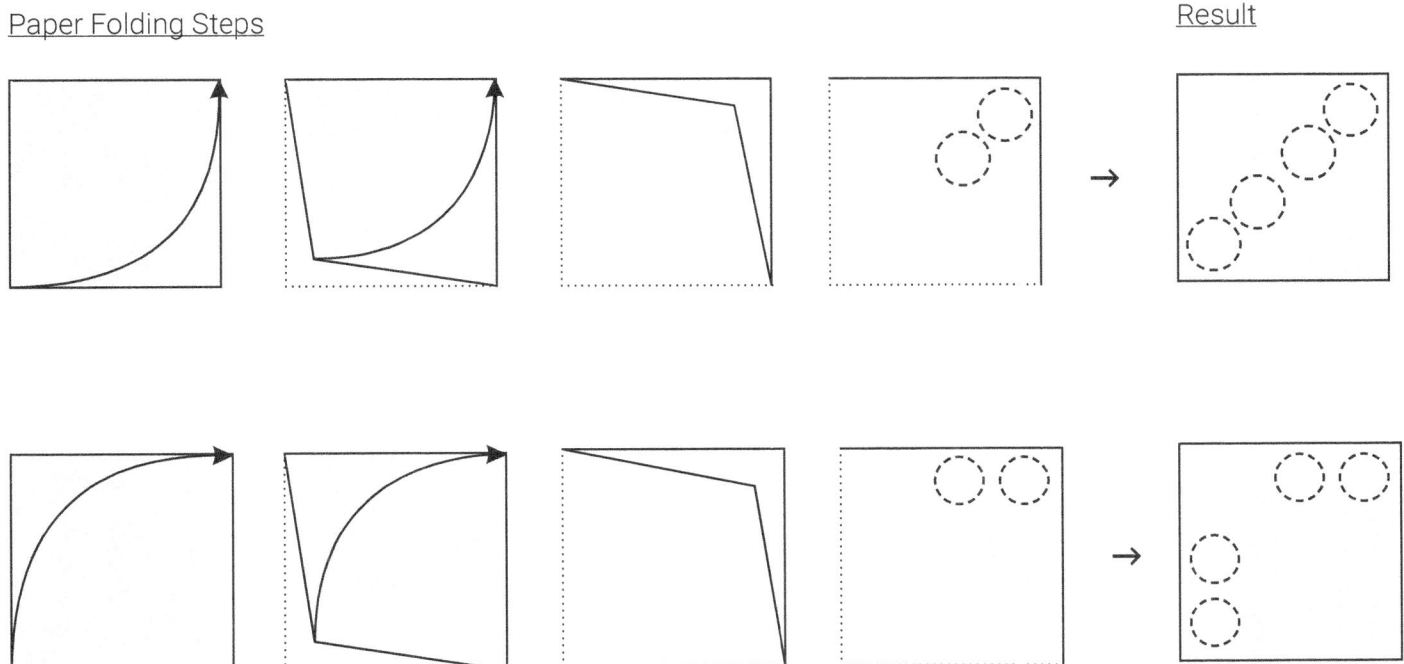

(In the question at the top of the page, the third choice is correct.)

Paper Folding Steps

In the example below, point out to your child that when the paper is unfolded the triangles point toward each other.

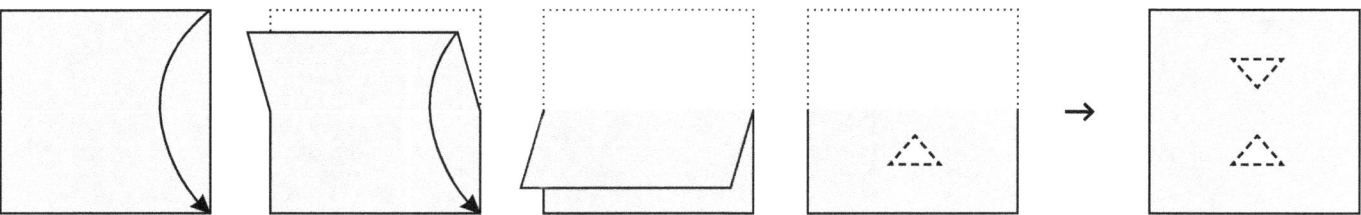

In the example below, point out to your child that the shape is cut into the fold line.

In the examples below, point out to your child how the paper is folded, and then folded again.

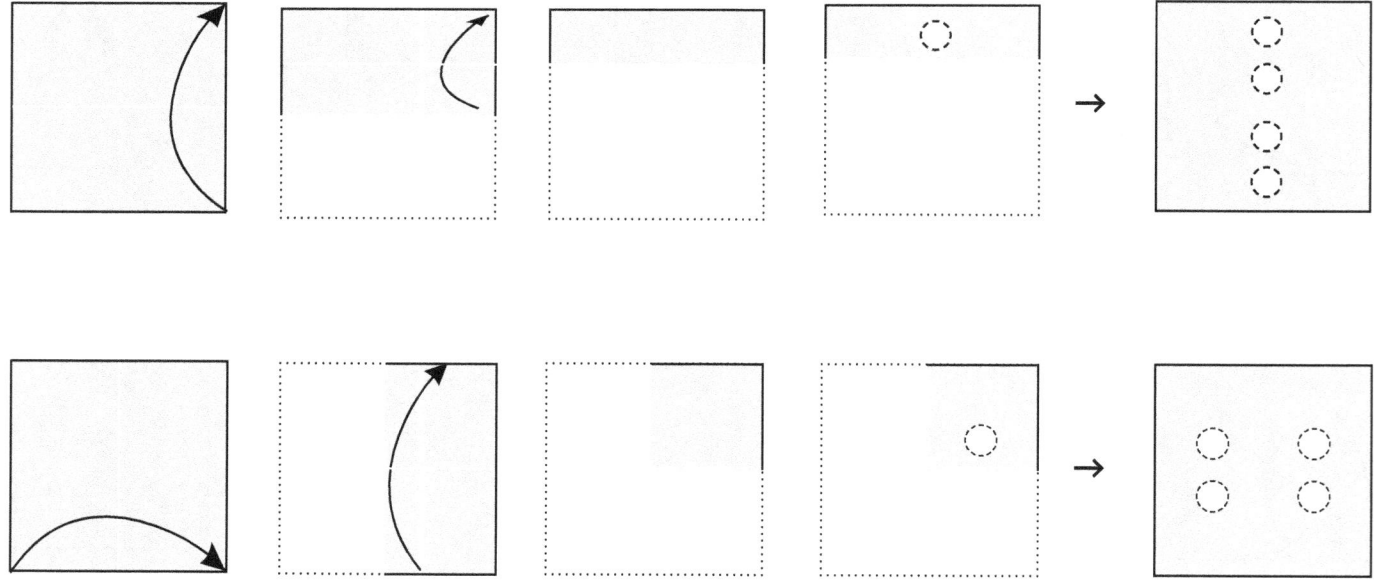

12

Parents, read the below with your child.

Watch out!

This book is filled with tricky questions. Can you answer them?

Of course you can!

Pay close attention to each question and try your best.

We'll be here to help you along the way!

Practice Test 1 (Workbook Format) begins on the next page.

FIGURE ANALOGIES

Sara

What goes in the empty box?

Directions (read to child): The pictures in the top boxes go together in some way. Look at the bottom boxes. One box is empty. Look at the row of pictures next to the boxes. These are the answer choices. Which one of these choices goes with the picture in the bottom box like the pictures in the top boxes go together?

Explanation (for parents): A more detailed explanation and a Figure Analogies example question is on p. 6. If you have not already, look over p. 6 (later). Try to define a "rule" to describe how the top set belongs together. With Figure Analogies, this "rule" could describe a "change" that occurs from the top left box to the top right box. Next, take this "rule" describing the change, and apply it to the bottom picture.

Example (read this to child): In the first box, we see a gray diamond. In the second box, we see a gray diamond, but this time a smaller white diamond is in the middle. Our rule is that the same gray shape from the first box is in the second box, but in the second box a smaller white version is in the middle.

Let's look in the bottom box. We see another gray shape. Which answer choice follows our rule? Find the choice that shows the same shape as the first box, but has a smaller white version in the middle. Choice C is the right answer.

1.

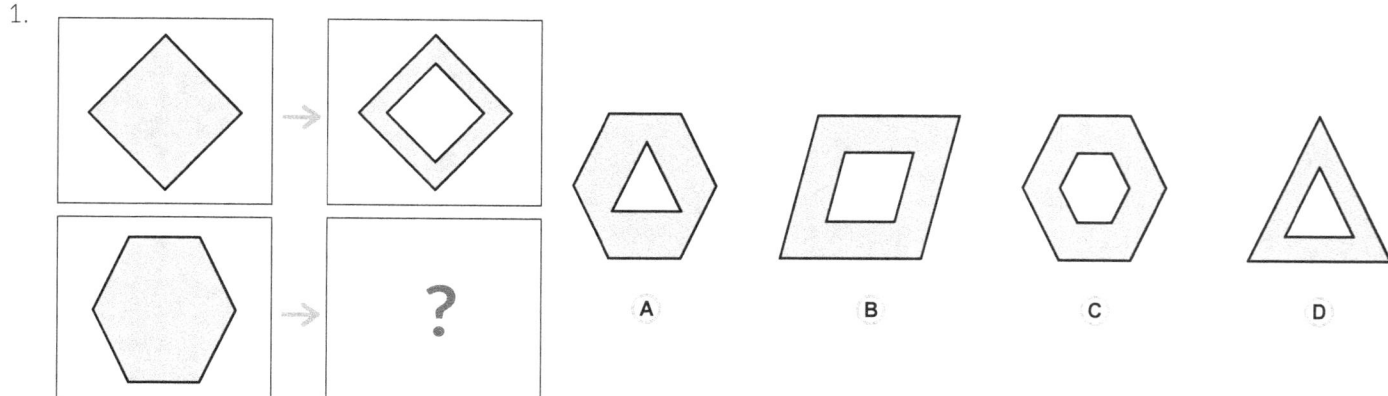

2.

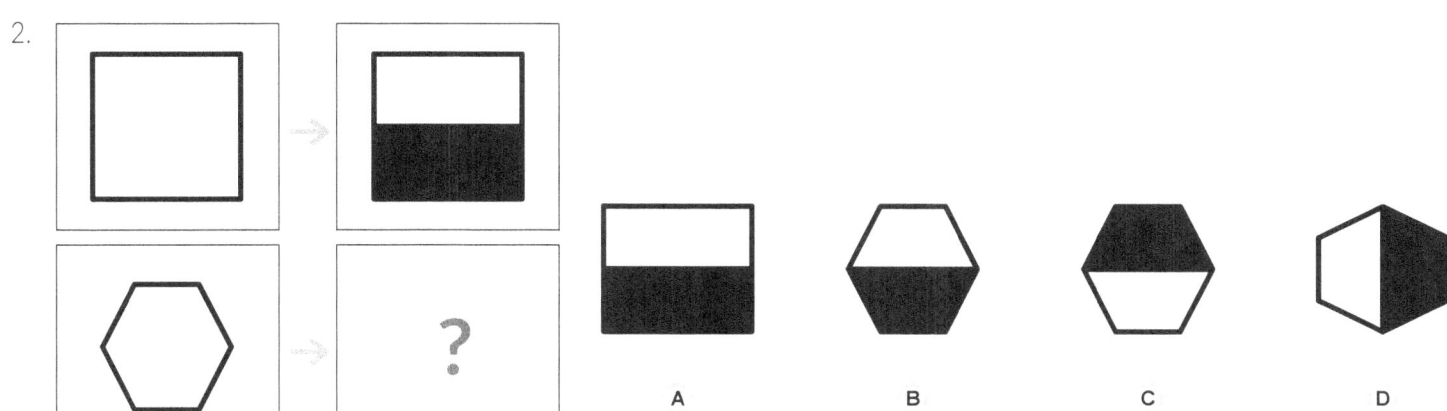

3.

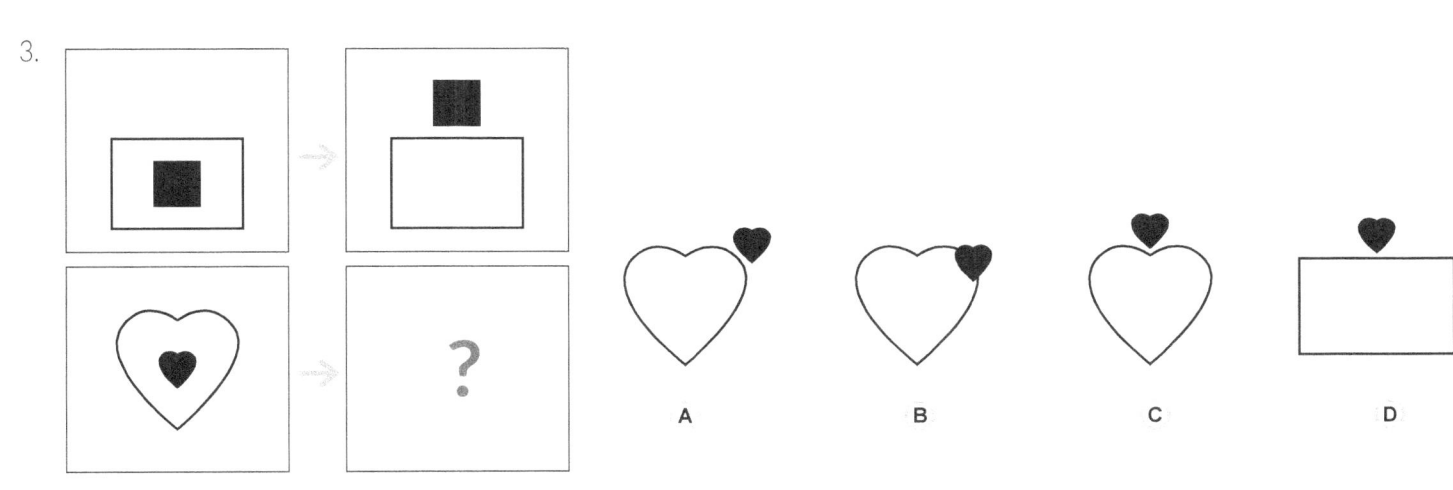

4.

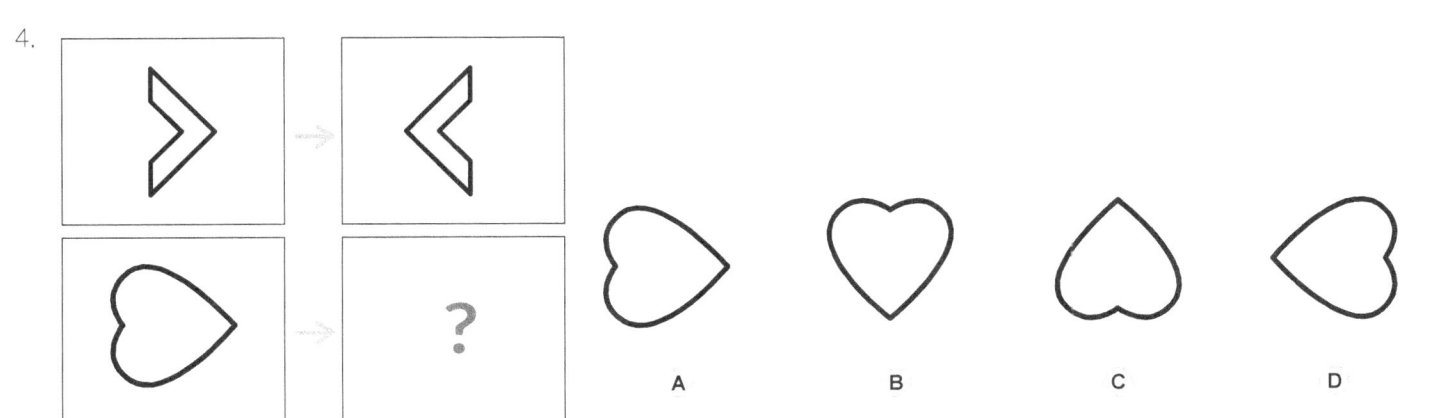

5.

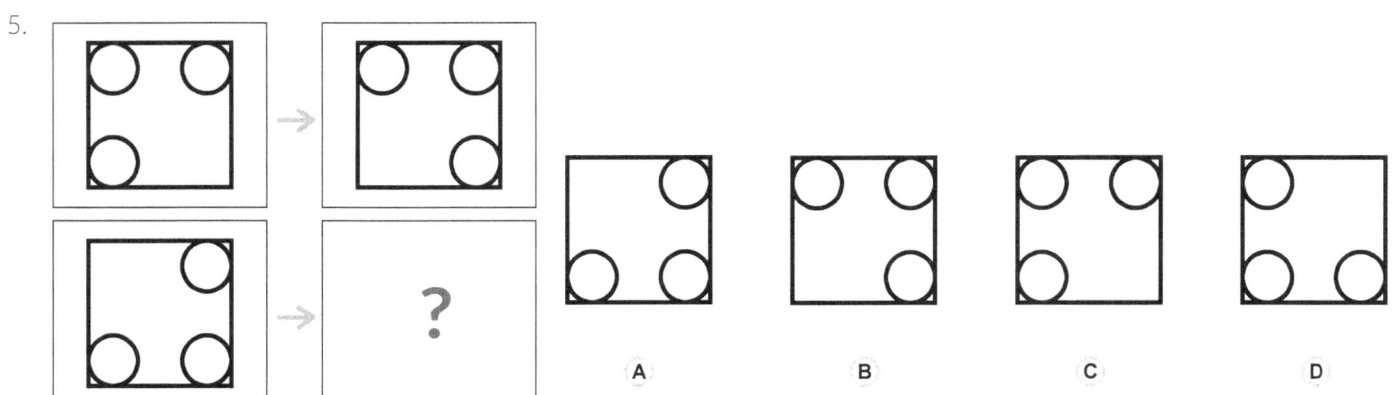

6.

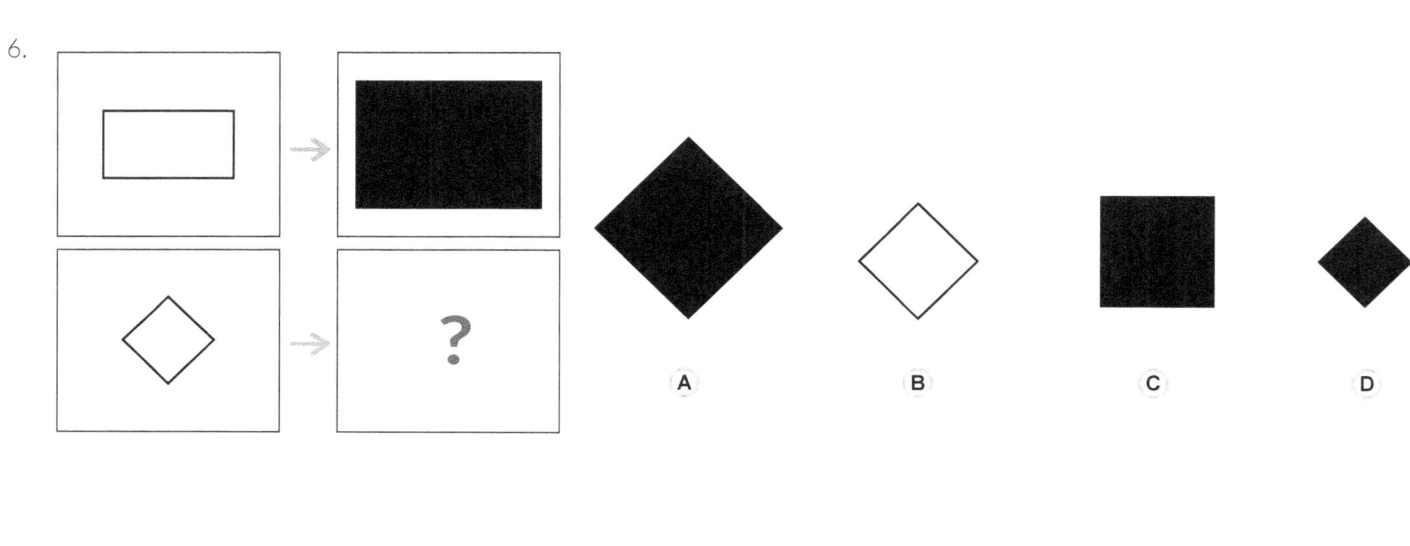

7.

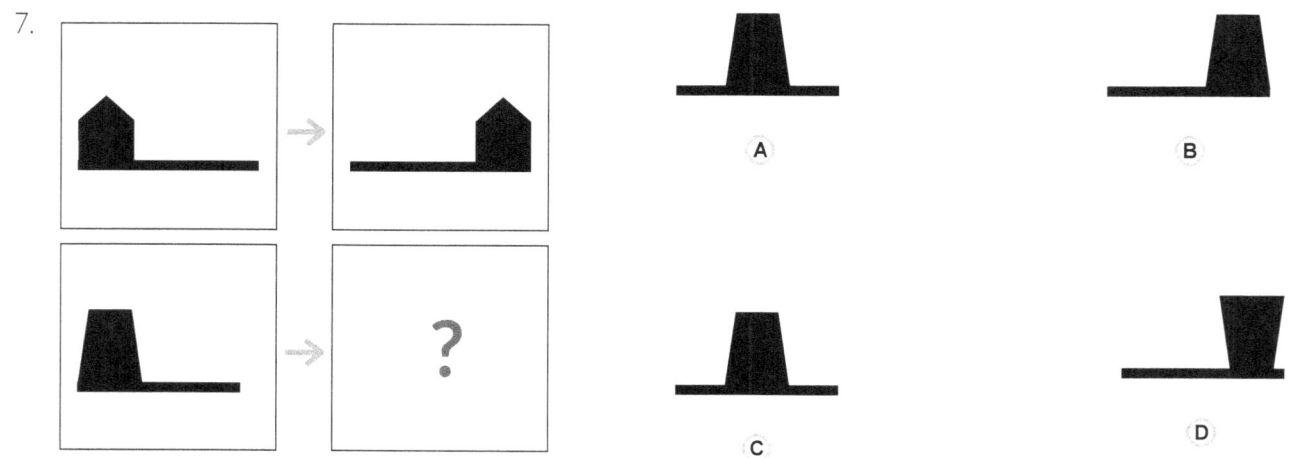

8.

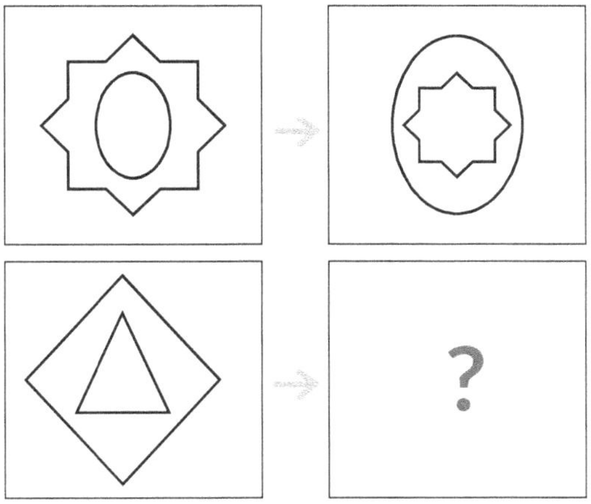

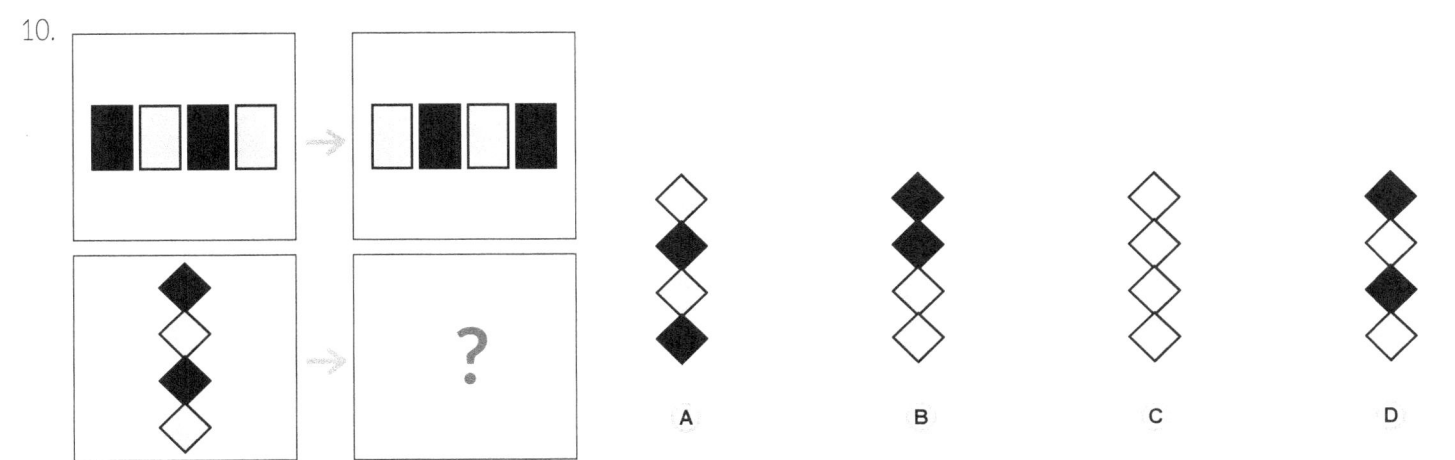

9.

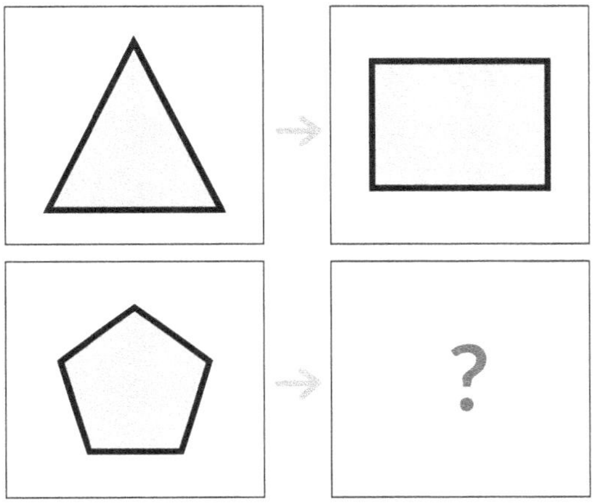

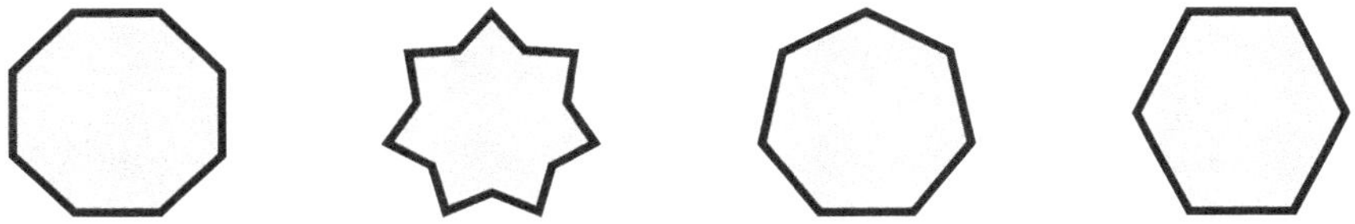

10.

11.

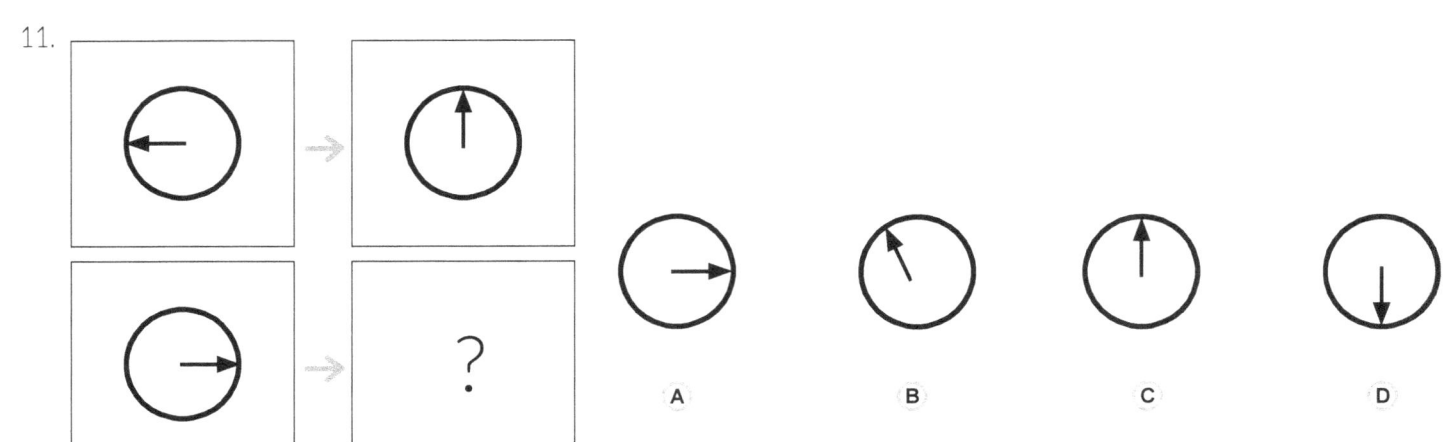

12.

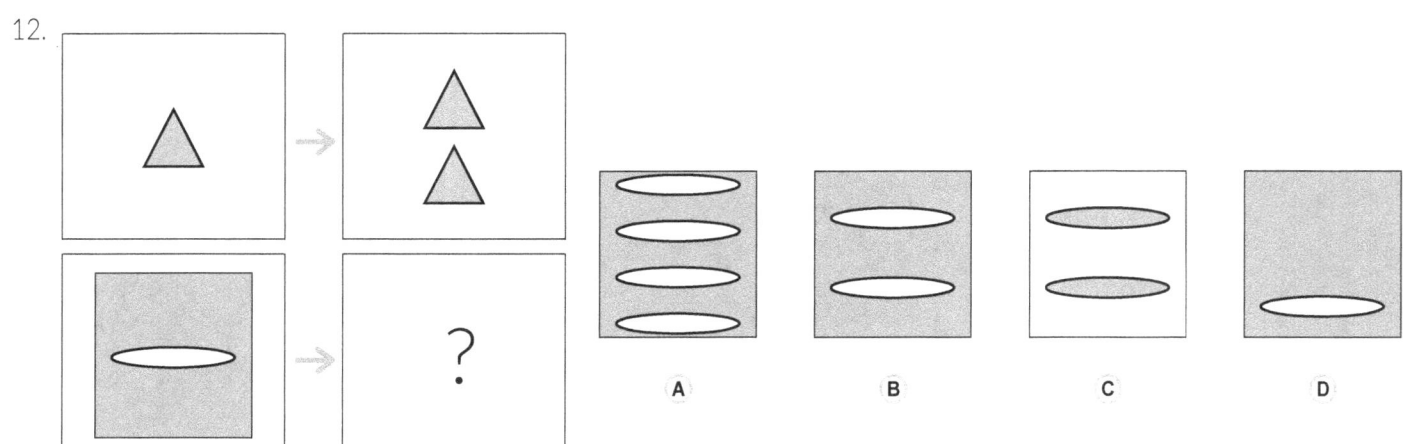

13.

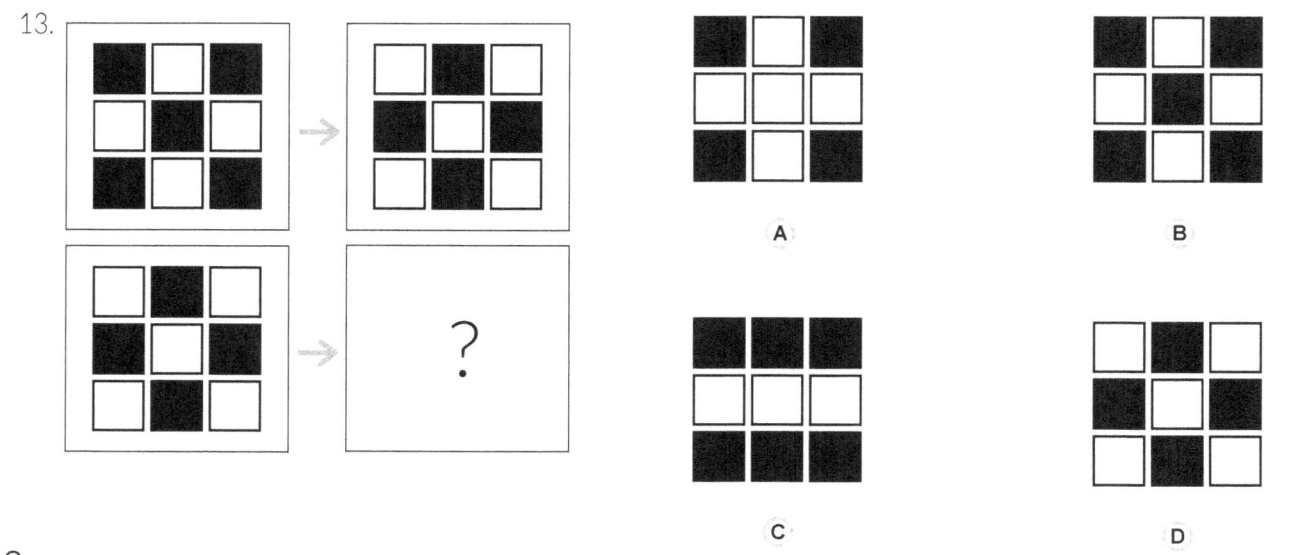

18

14.

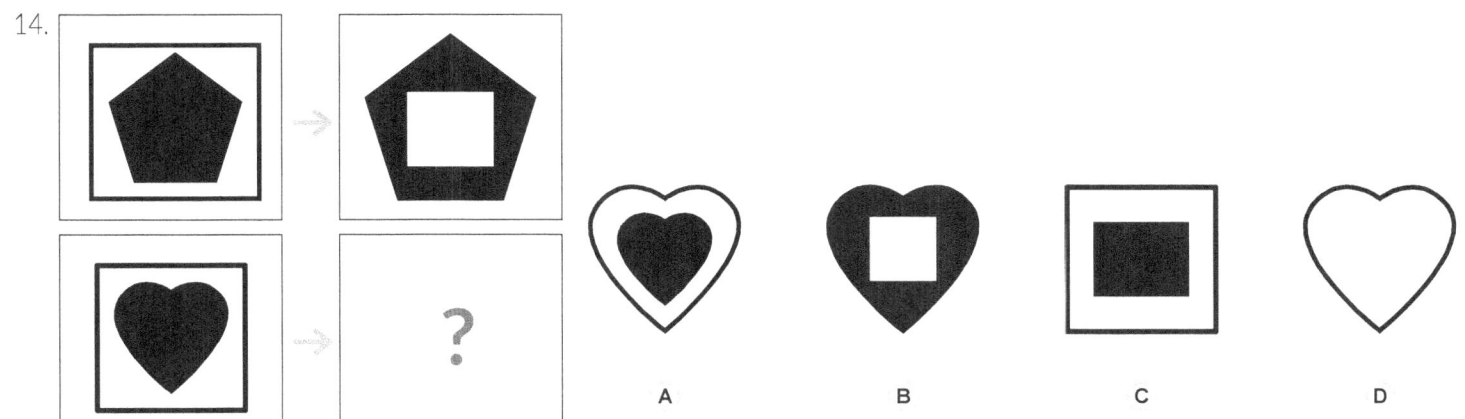

15.

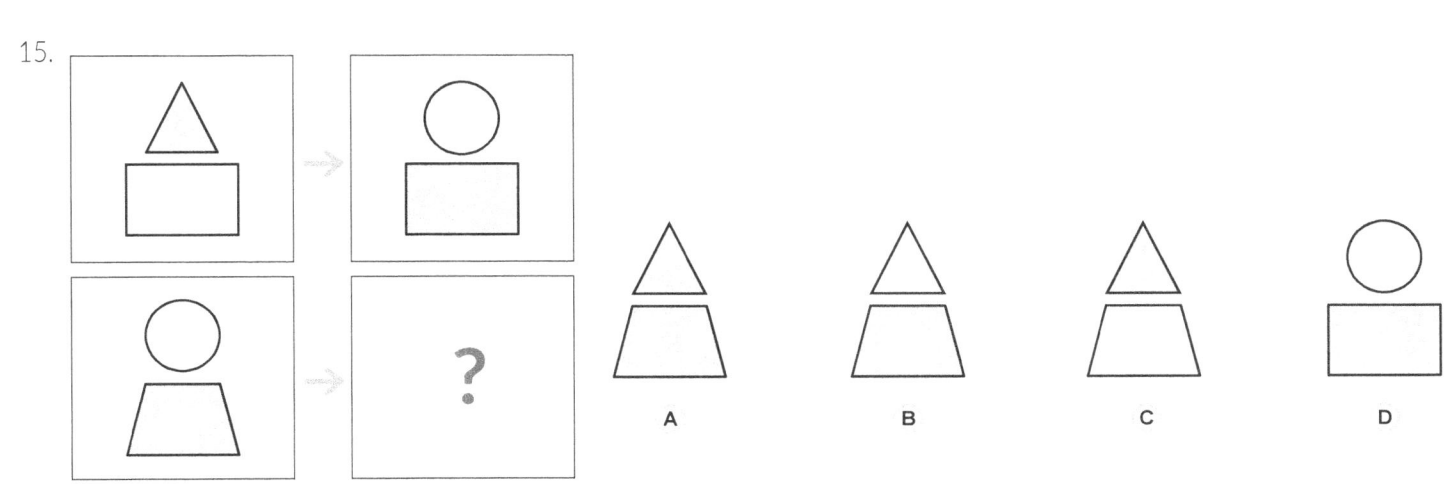

16.

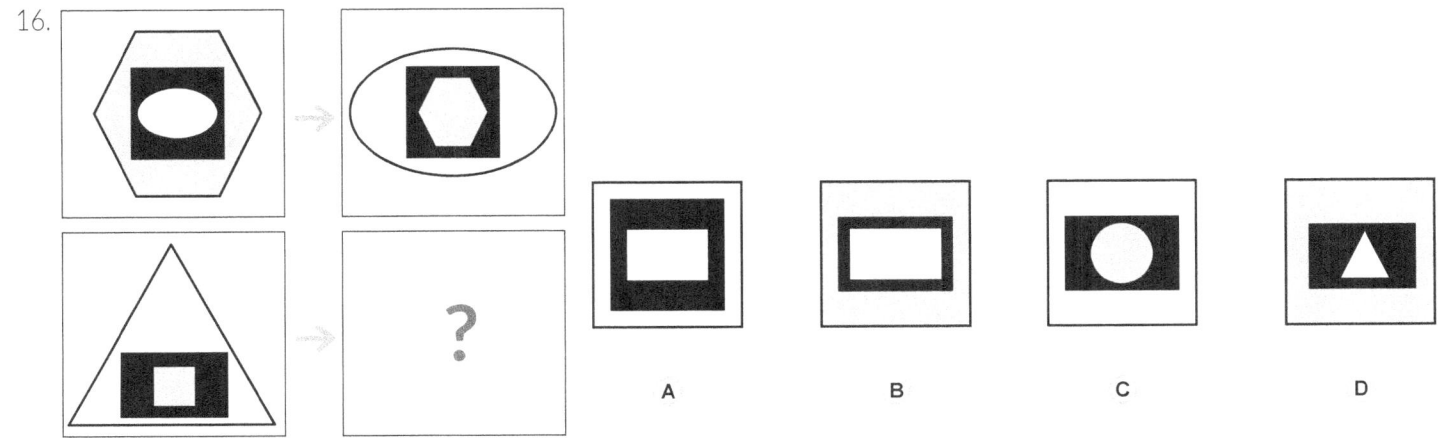

19

17.

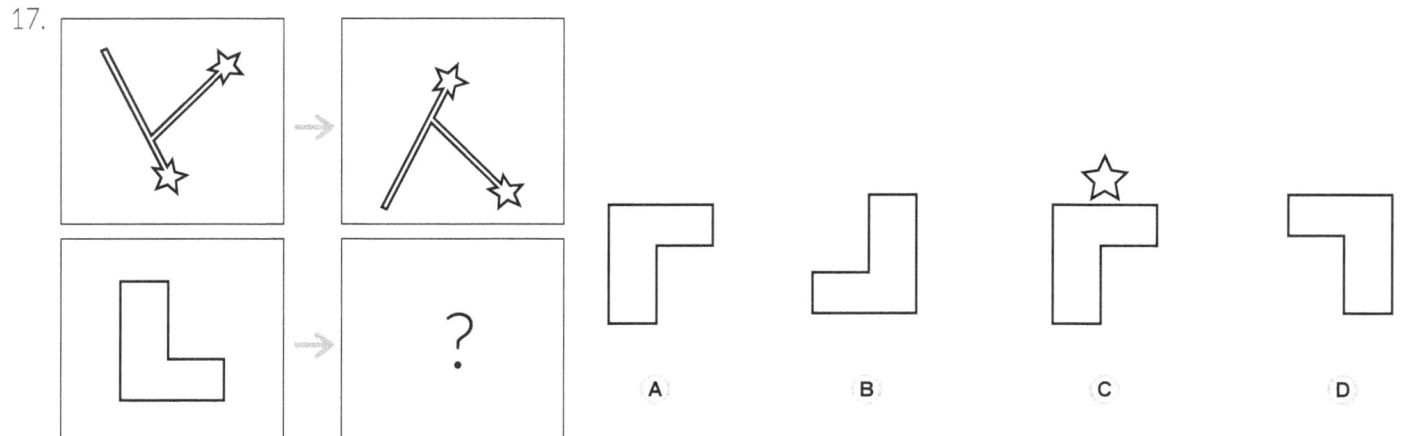

18.

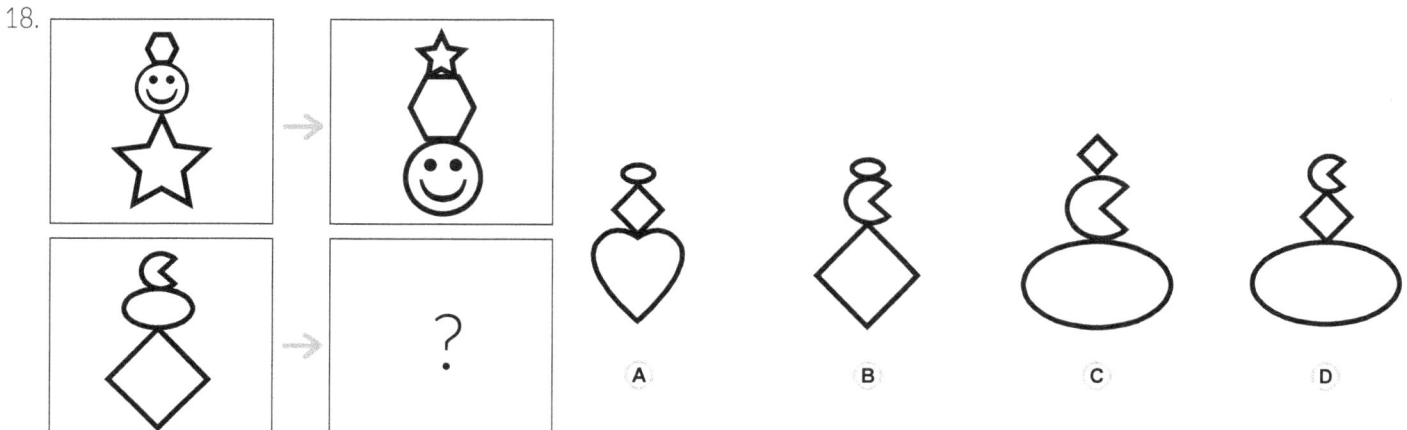

Keep up the good work!

Jay

FIGURE CLASSIFICATION

Kai

Directions (read to child): The top row shows three pictures that are alike in some way. Look at the bottom row. There are four pictures. Which picture in the bottom row goes best with the pictures in the top row?

Explanation (for parents): A more detailed explanation of Figure Classification questions is on p.8. If you have not already, look over p. 8 (later). Following is an excerpt.

Together with your child, try to figure out a "rule" describing how the top pictures are alike and belong together. Then, apply the "rule" to each answer choice to determine which one follows it.

If your child finds that more than one choice follows the rule, then a more specific rule is needed.

The "rule" for number 1 would be "the shape is a trapezoid." Choice C is the answer.

1.

| A | B | C | D |

2.

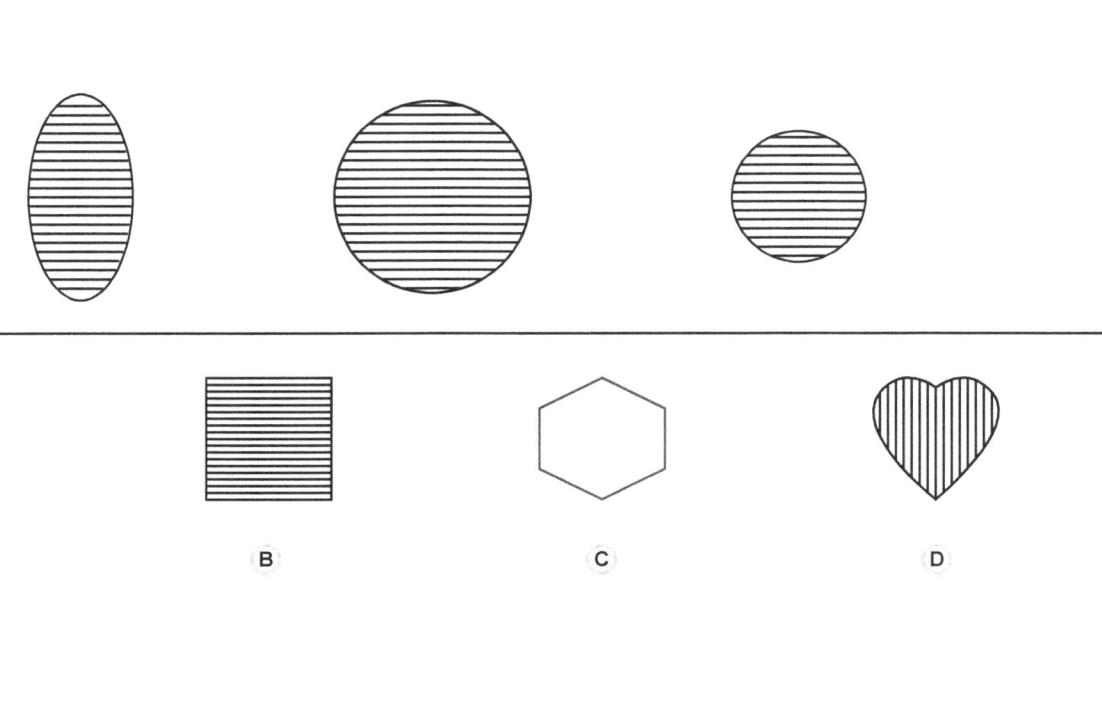

A B C D

3.

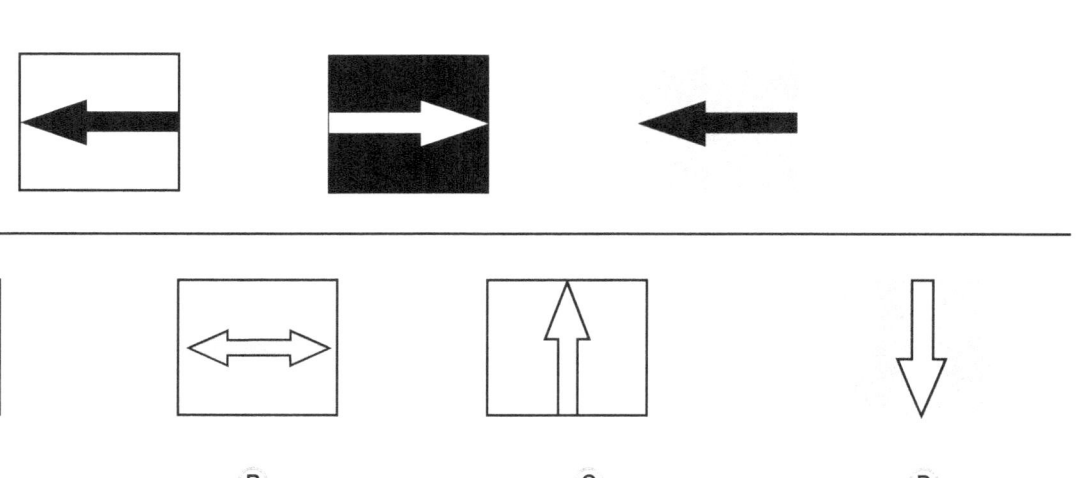

A B C D

4.

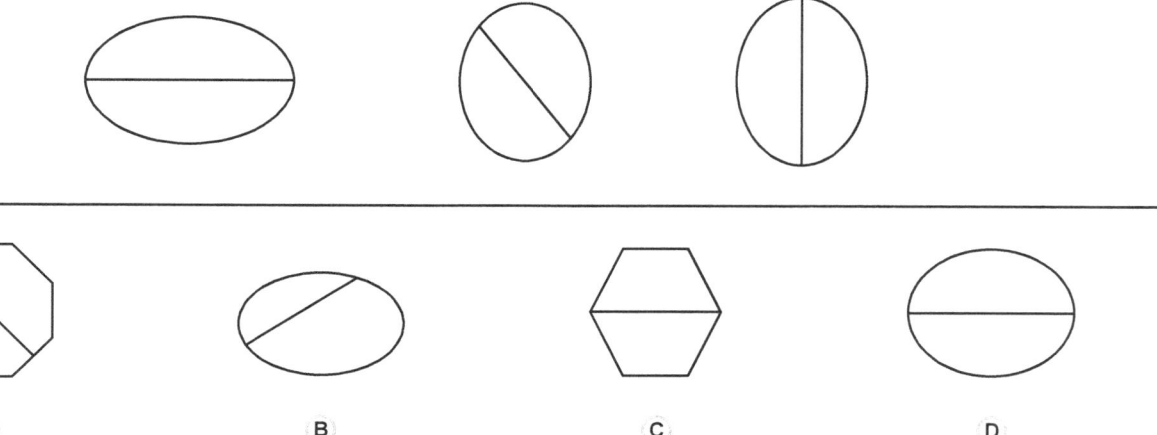

A B C D

5.

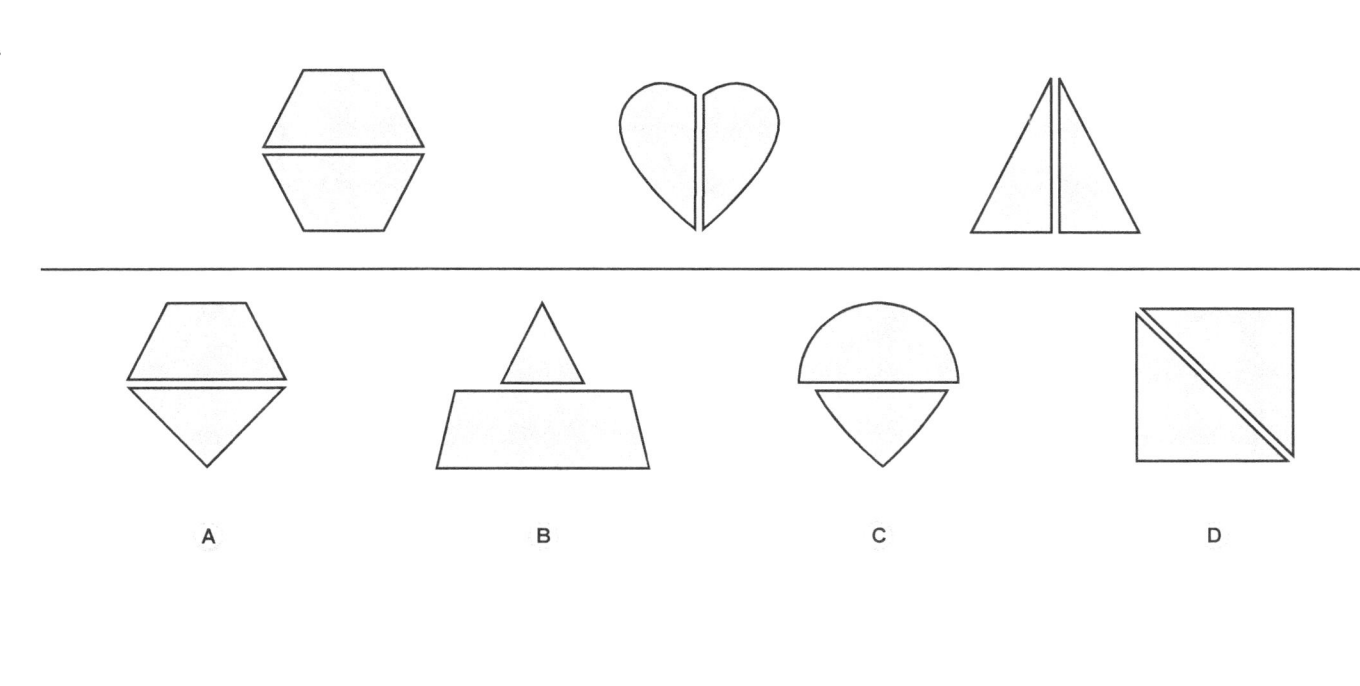

A   B   C   D

6.

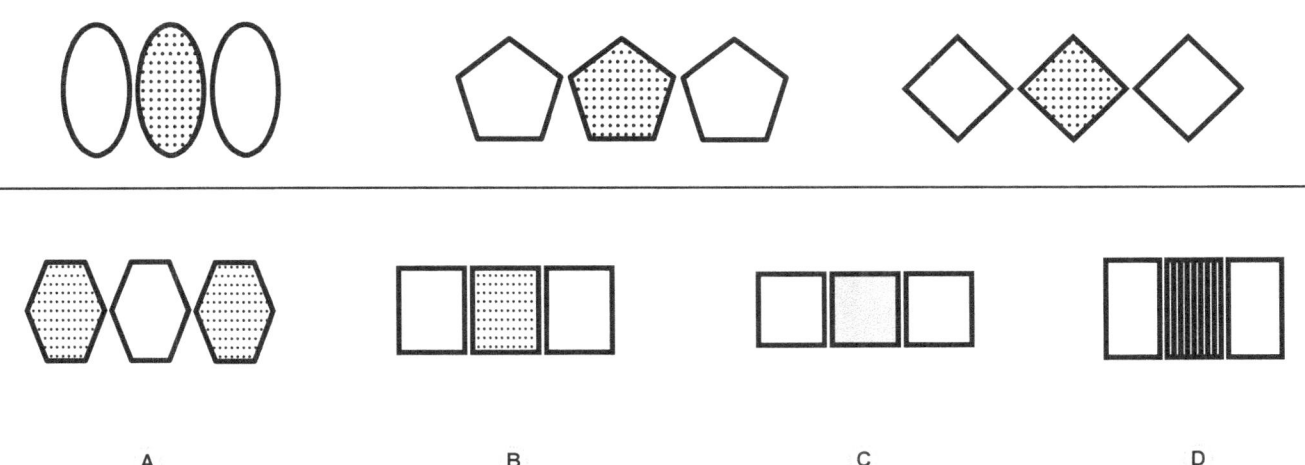

A   B   C   D

7.

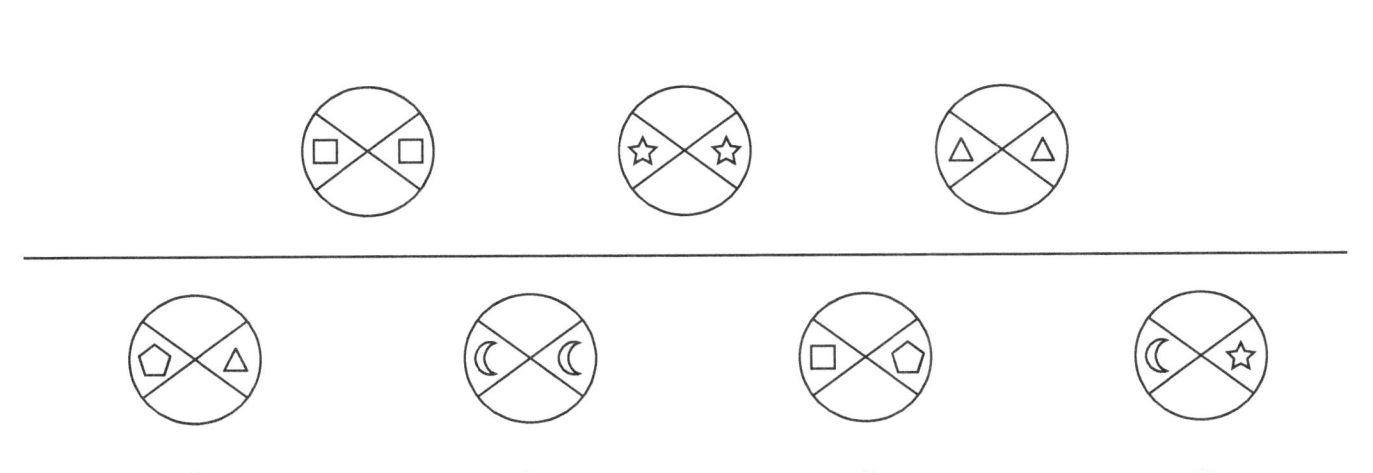

A   B   C   D

8.

A   B   C   D

9.

A   B   C   D

10.

A   B   C   D

11.

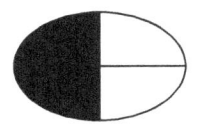 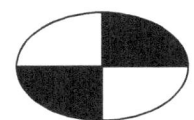 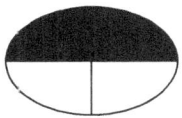

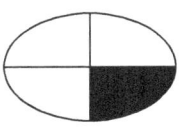

A   B   C   D

12.

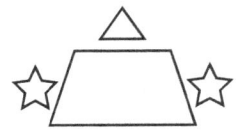 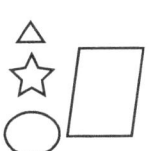

 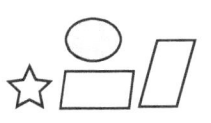 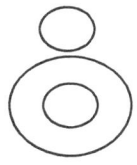

A   B   C   D

13.

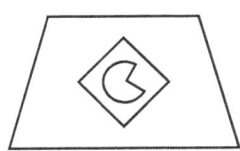 

 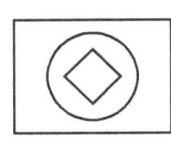 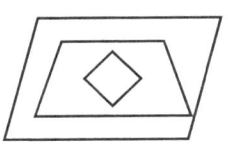 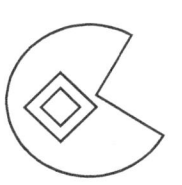

A   B   C   D

14.

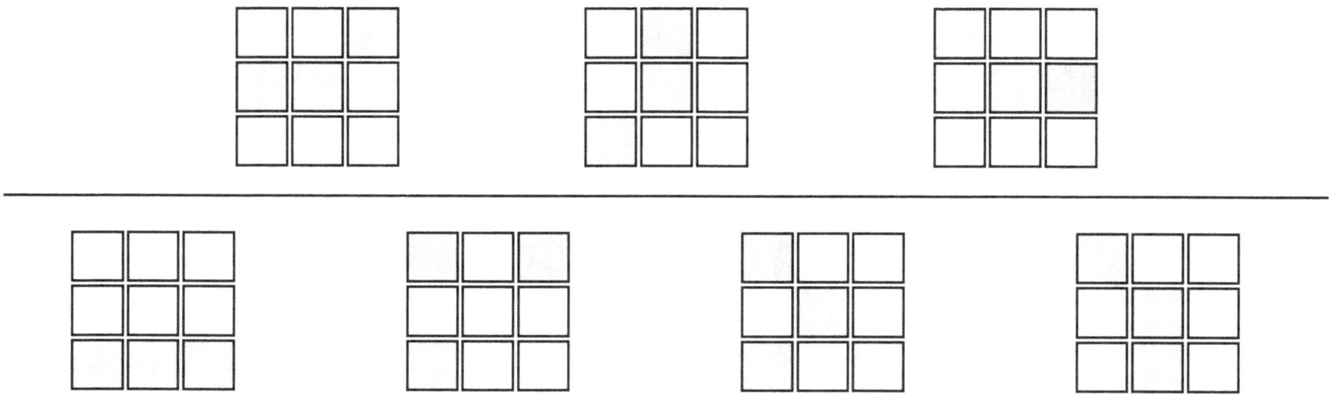

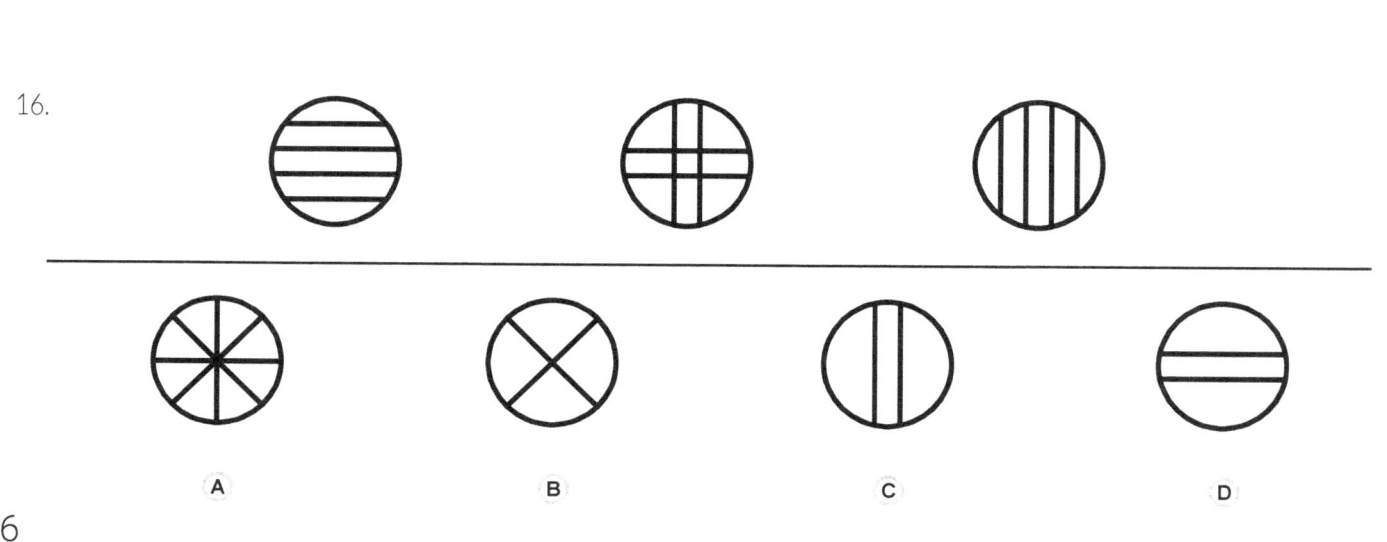

15.

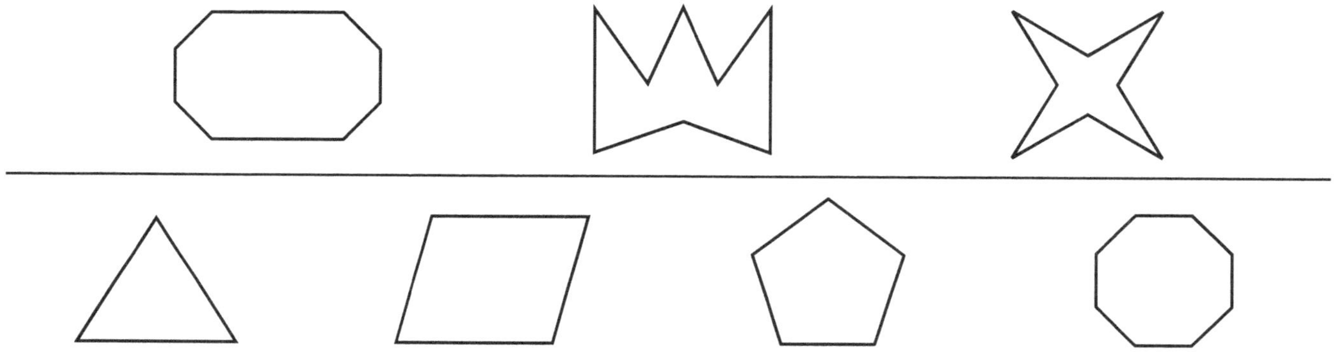

16.

17.

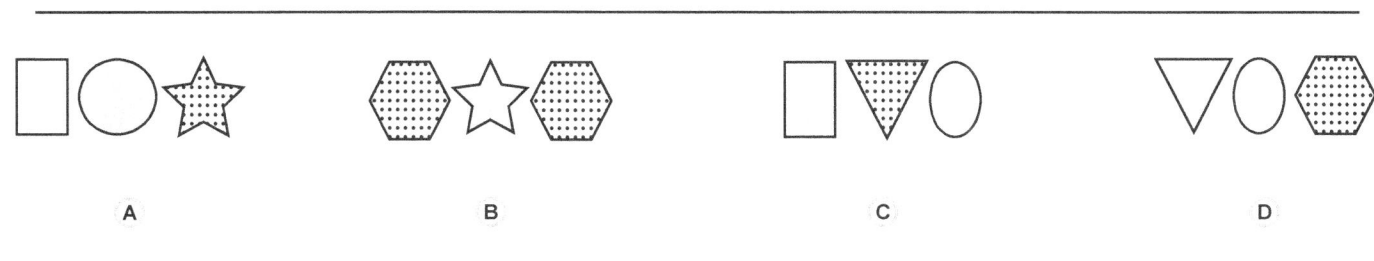

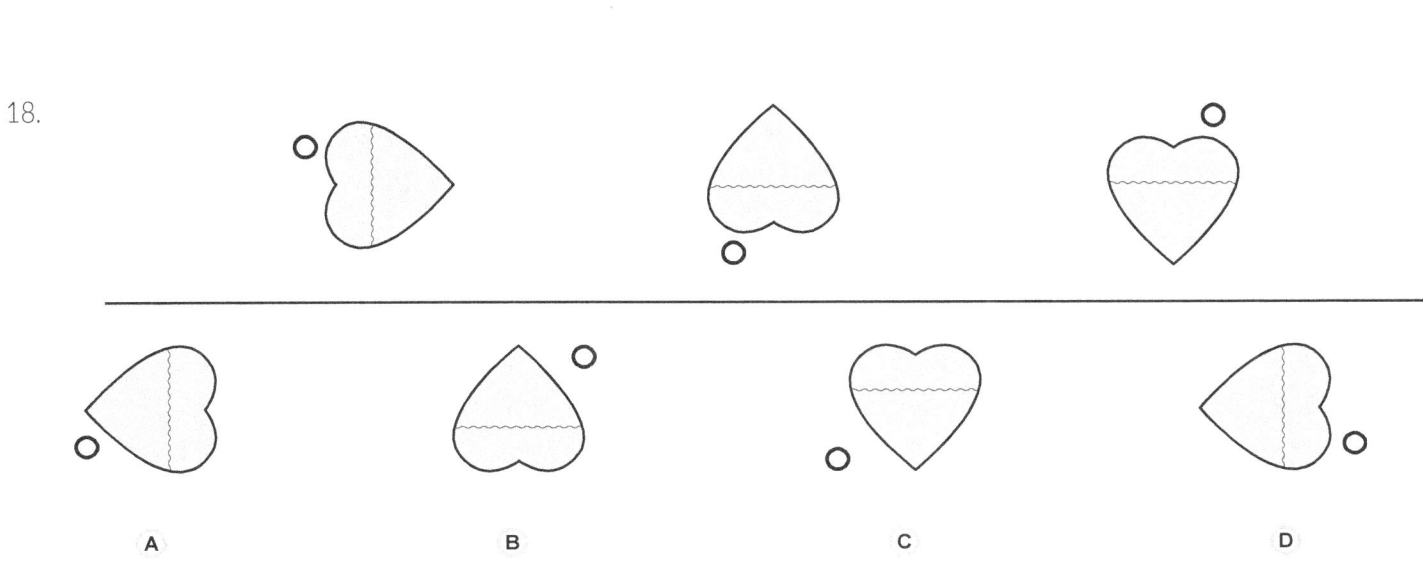

A   B   C   D

18.

PAPER FOLDING

Look closely!

Maya

Directions (read to child): The top row of pictures shows a sheet of paper. The paper was folded, then something was cut out. Which picture in the bottom row shows how the paper would look after it's unfolded?

Additional information (for parents): As explained earlier on p. 11, children may be initially "stumped" by Paper Folding. If your child needs help, then try demonstrating with real paper and a hole puncher.

Be sure to point out the number of holes made and their position after opening the paper.

1.

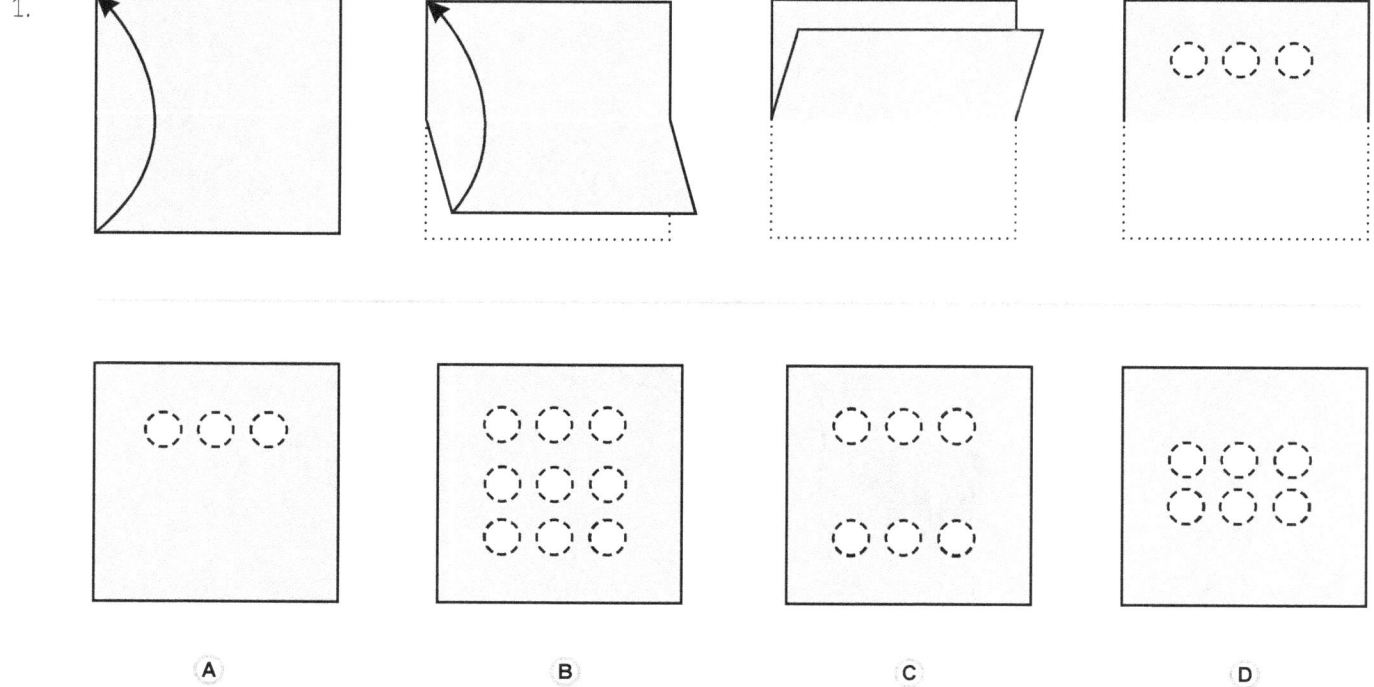

A   B   C   D

2.

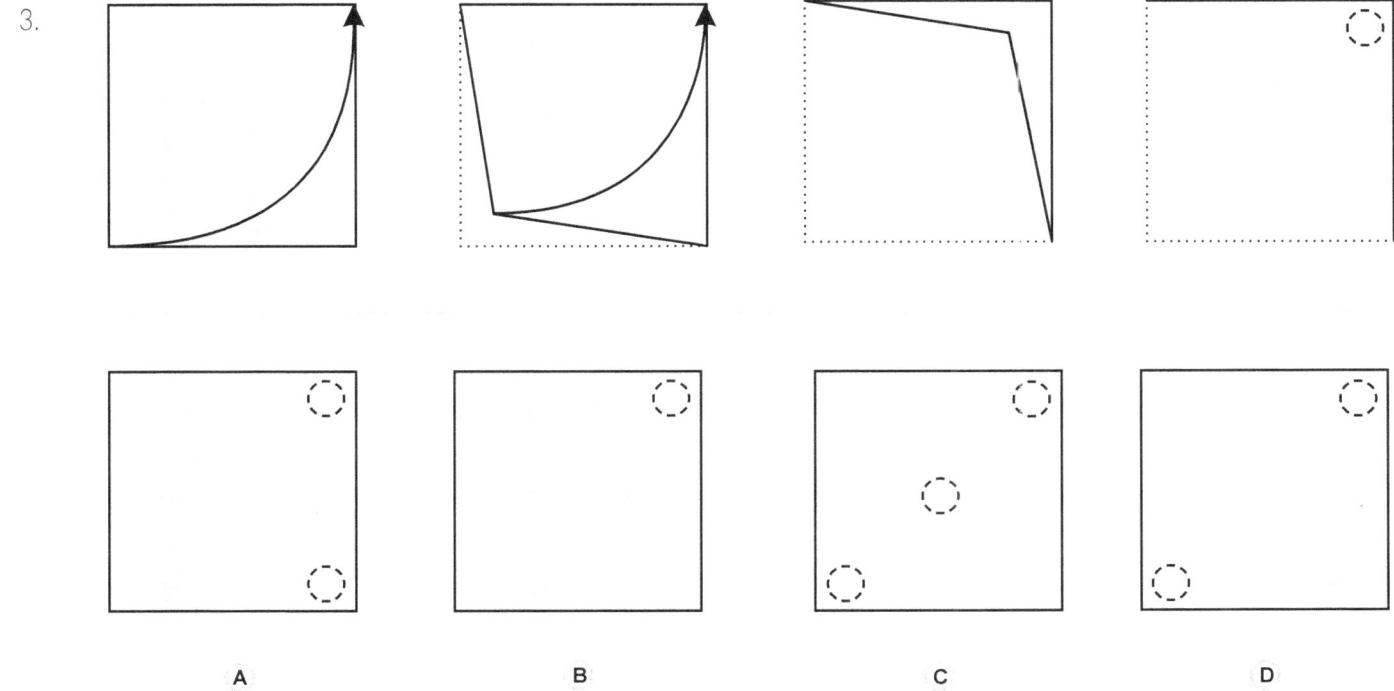

A   B   C   D

3.

A   B   C   D

4.

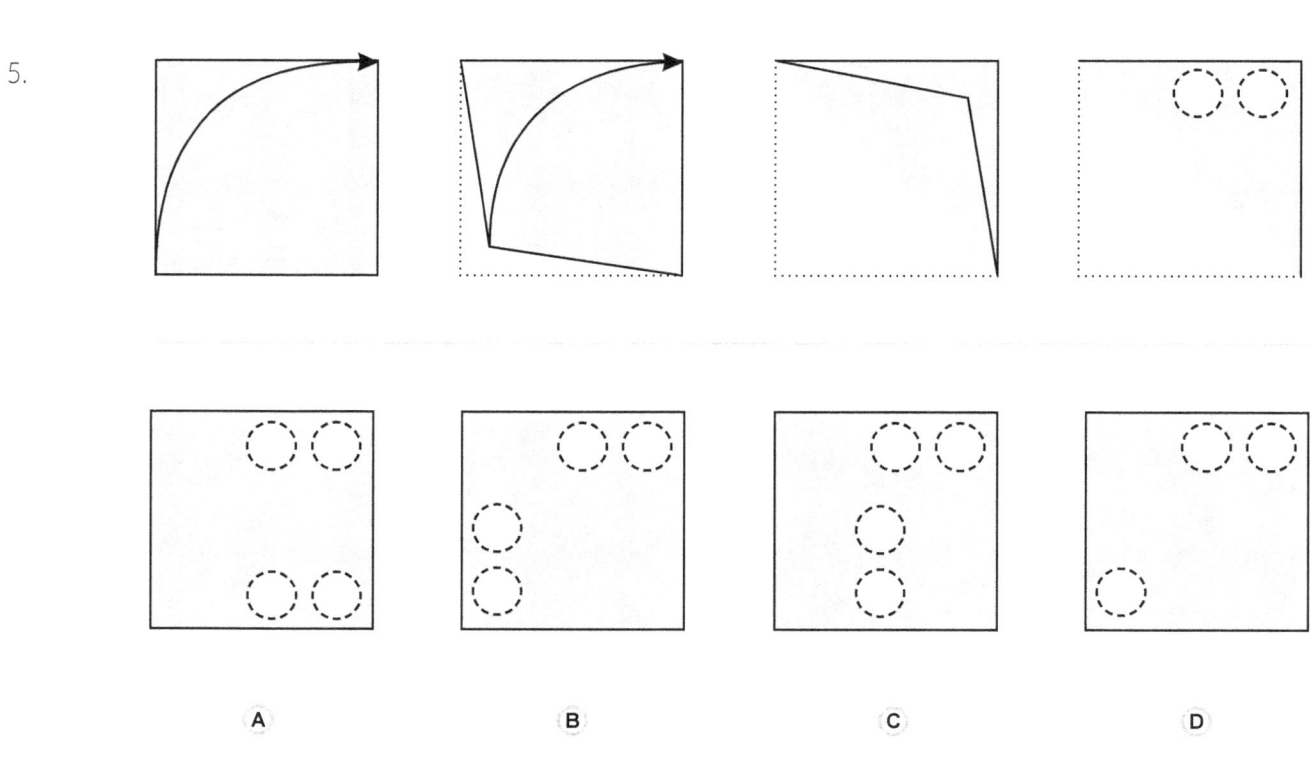

A   B   C   D

5.

A   B   C   D

30

6.

7.

A   B   C   D

Note: In the next questions, the paper is folded twice. Point this out to your child.

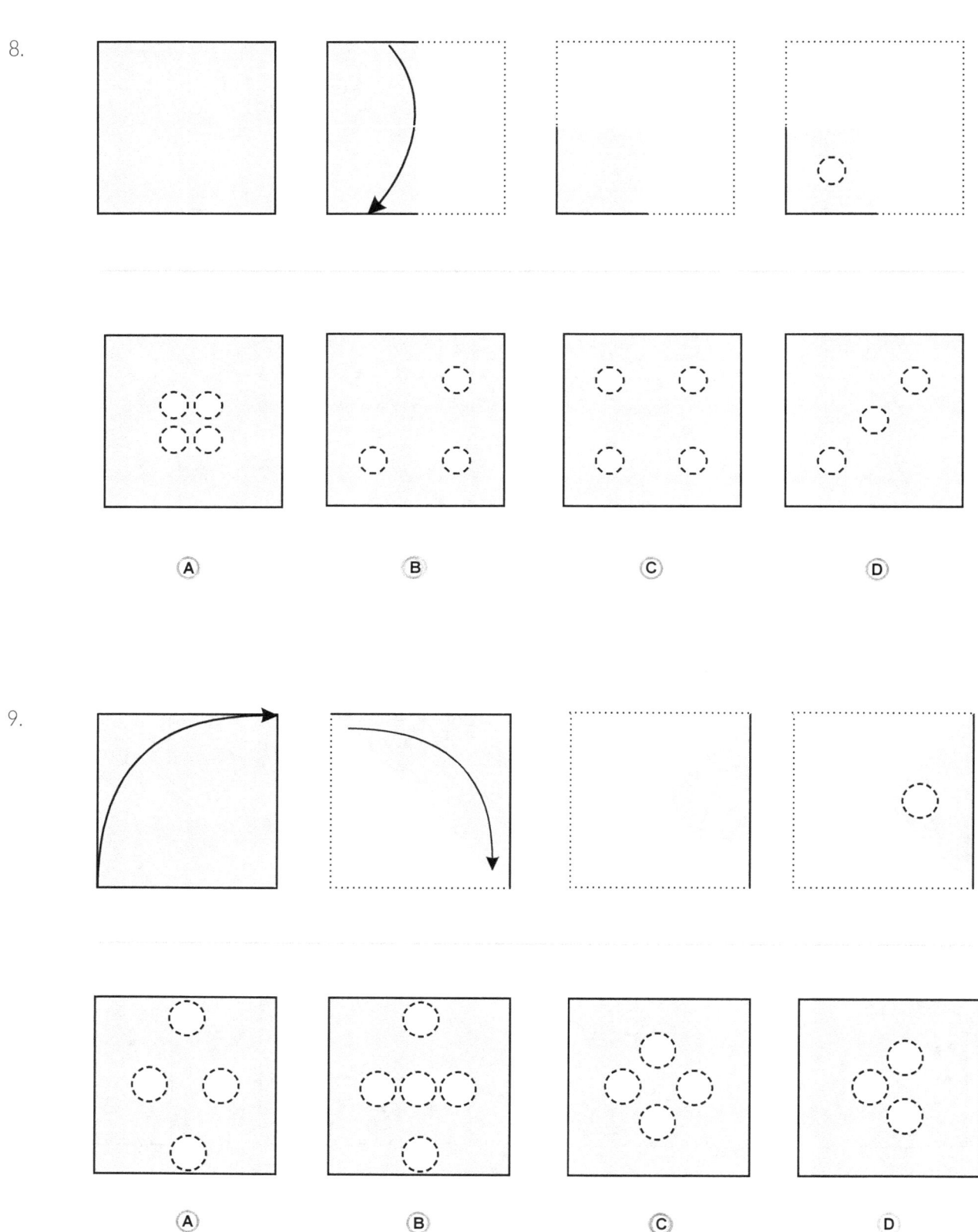

8.

 A   B   C   D

9.

 A   B   C   D

10.

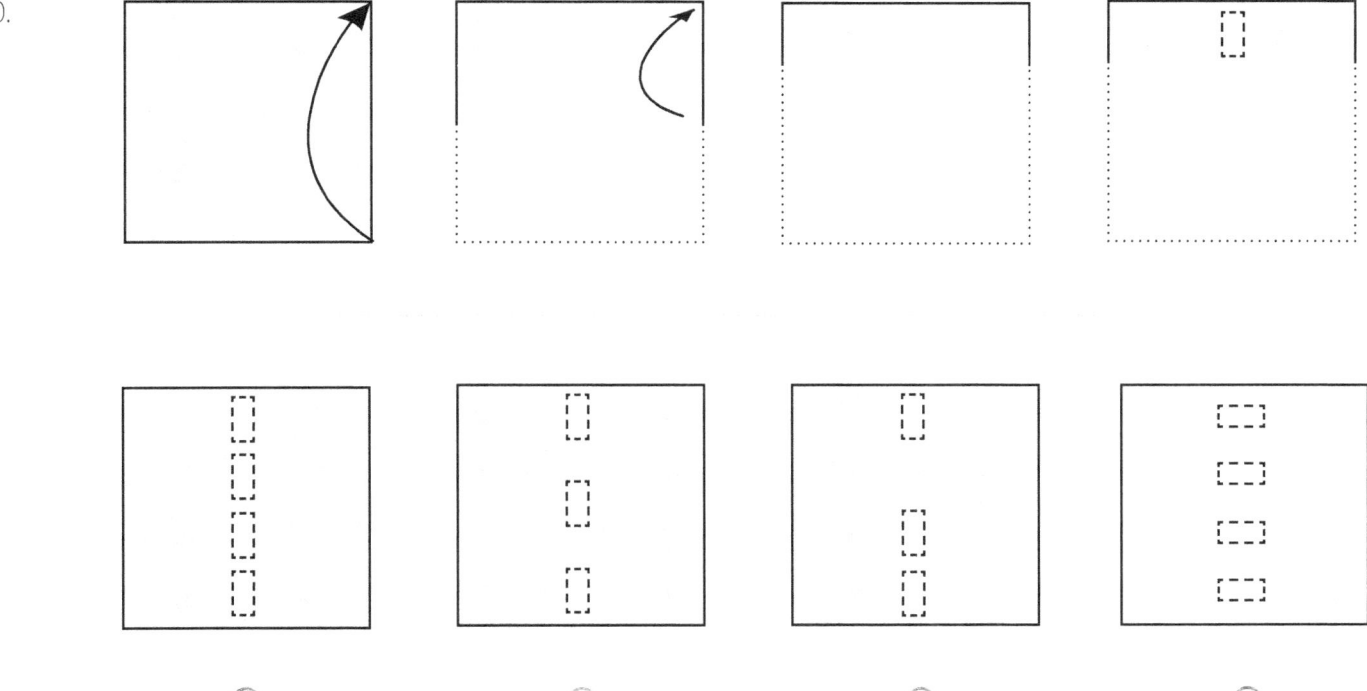

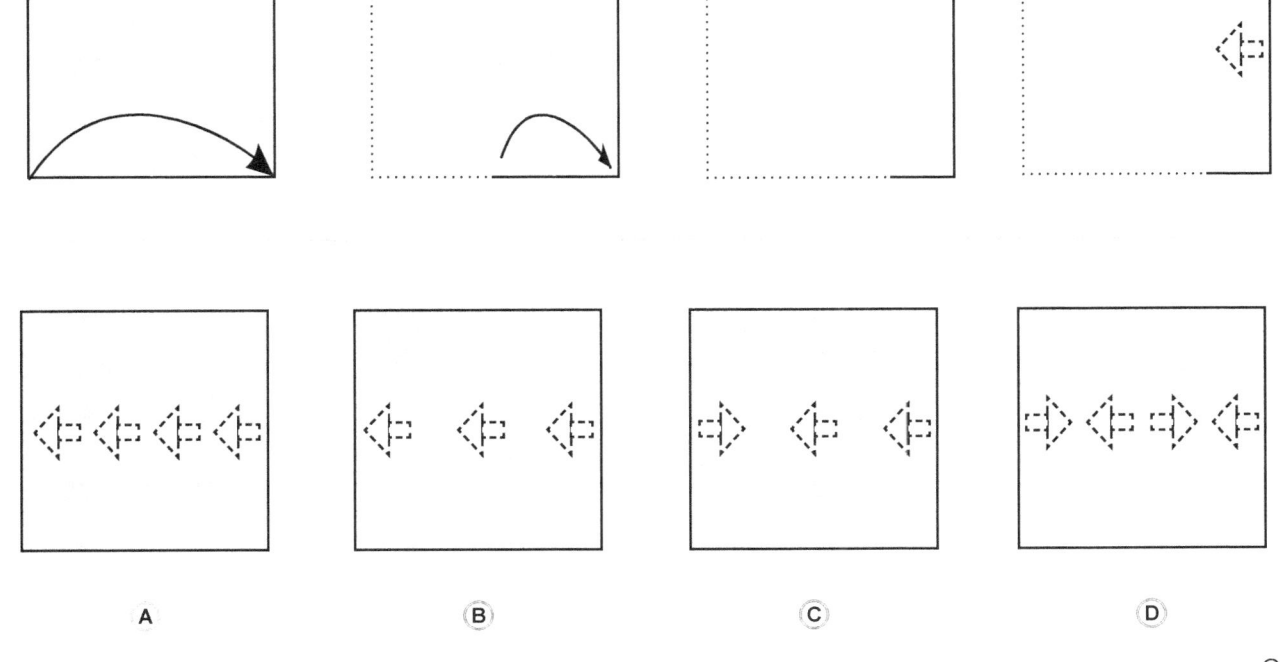

11.

12.

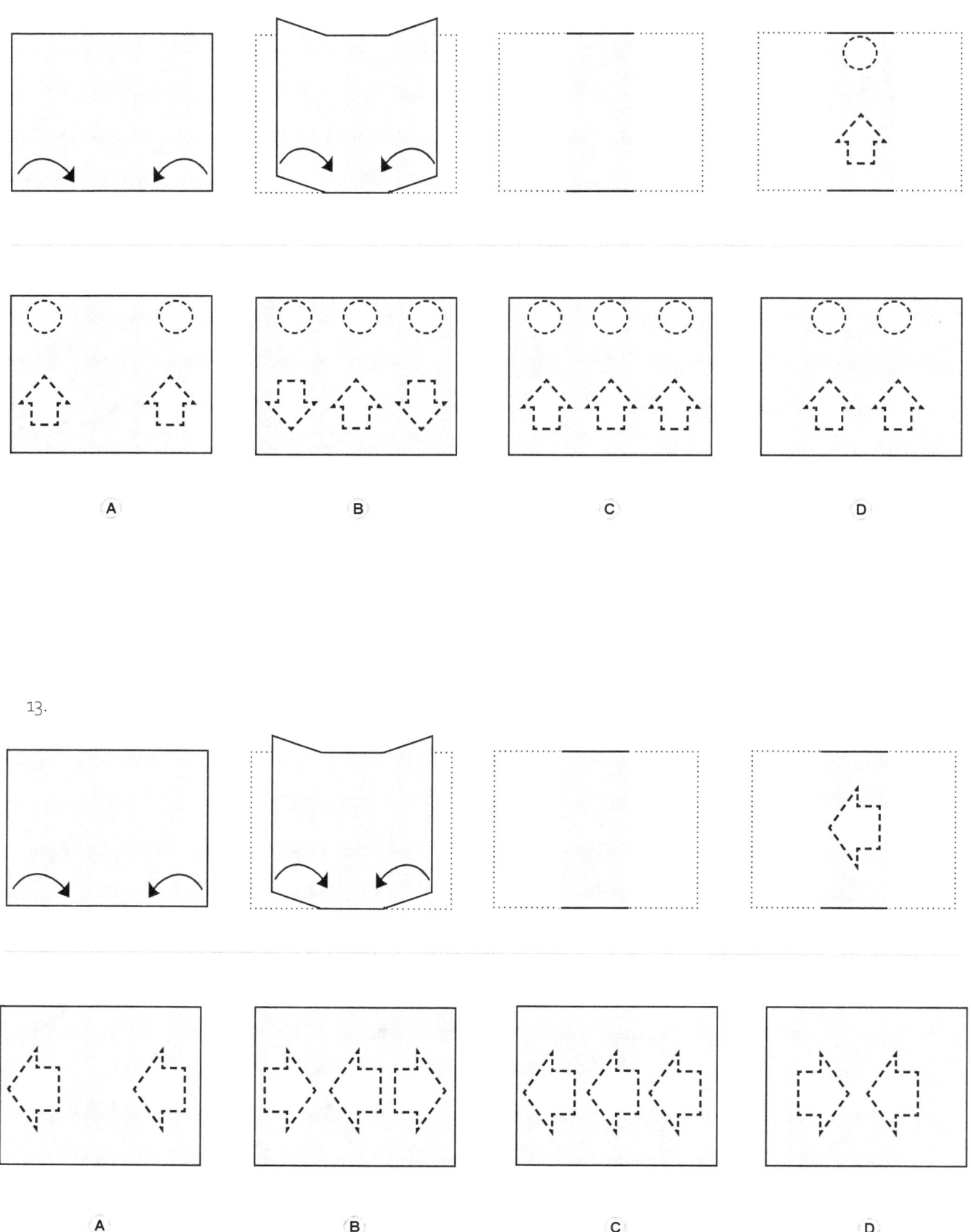

A B C D

13.

34

14.

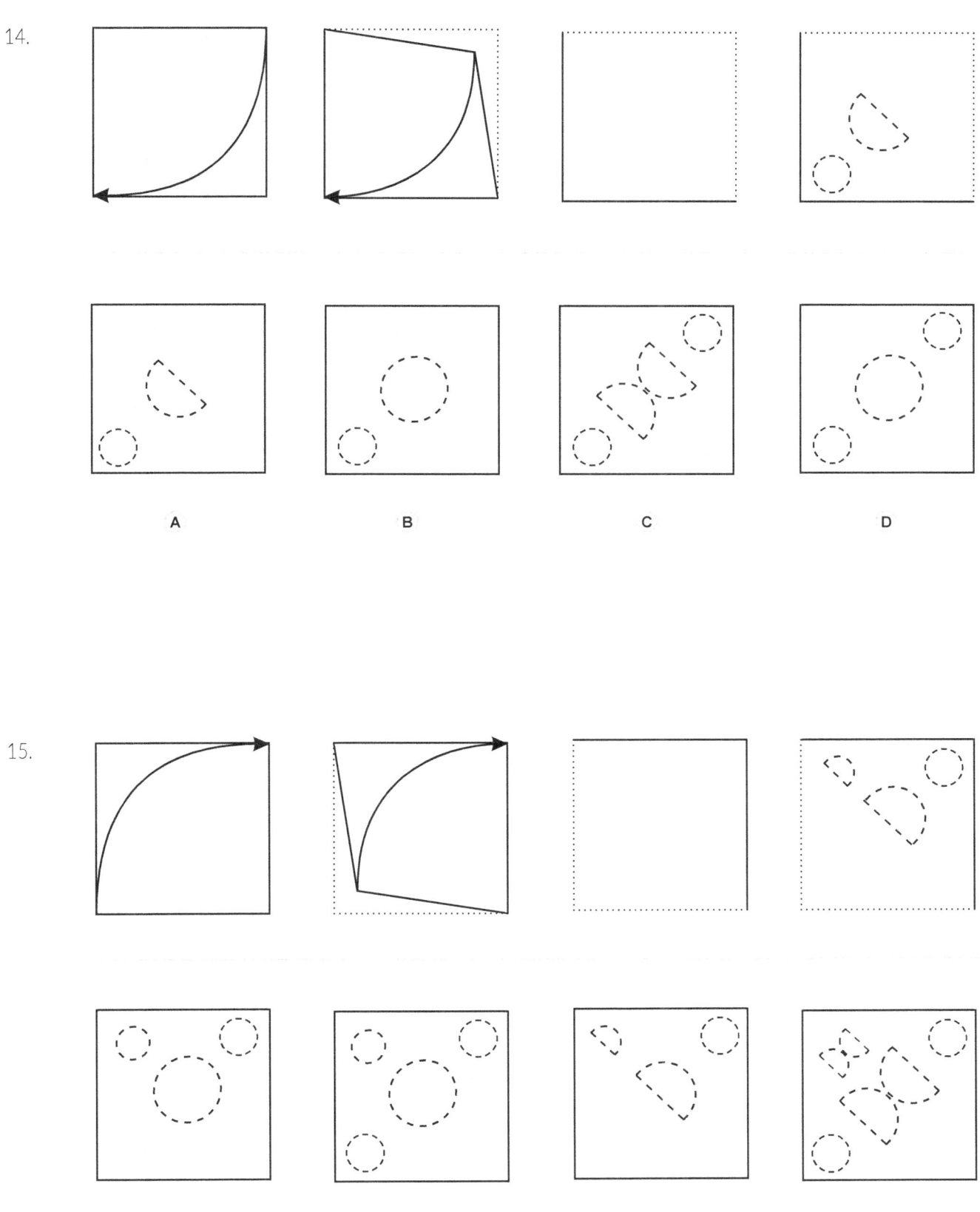

A   B   C   D

15.

A   B   C   D

16.

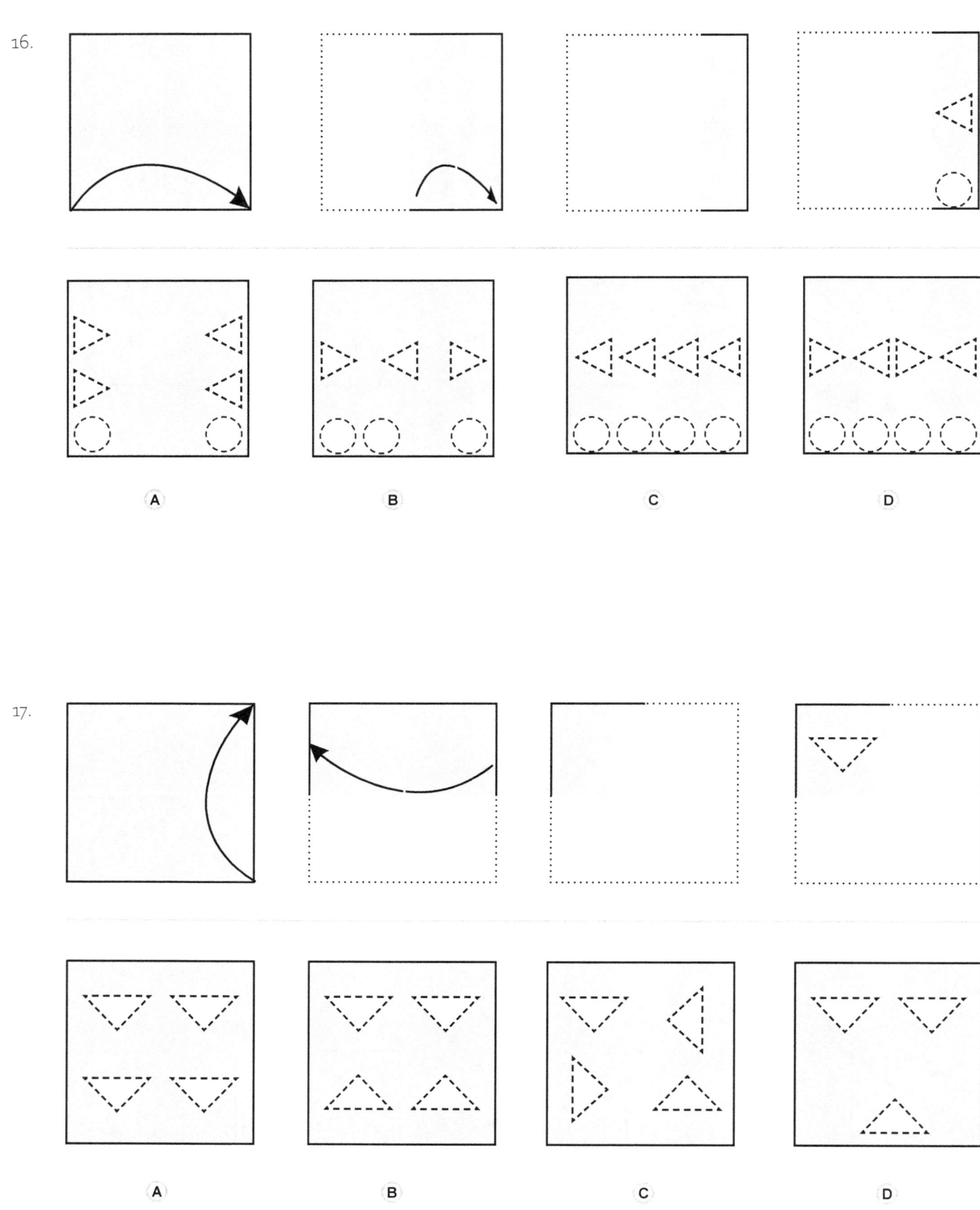

A   B   C   D

17.

A   B   C   D

COGAT® PRACTICE TEST 2

Directions: The pictures in the top boxes go together in some way. One of the bottom boxes is empty. Which answer choice goes with the picture in the bottom box in the same way the top pictures do?

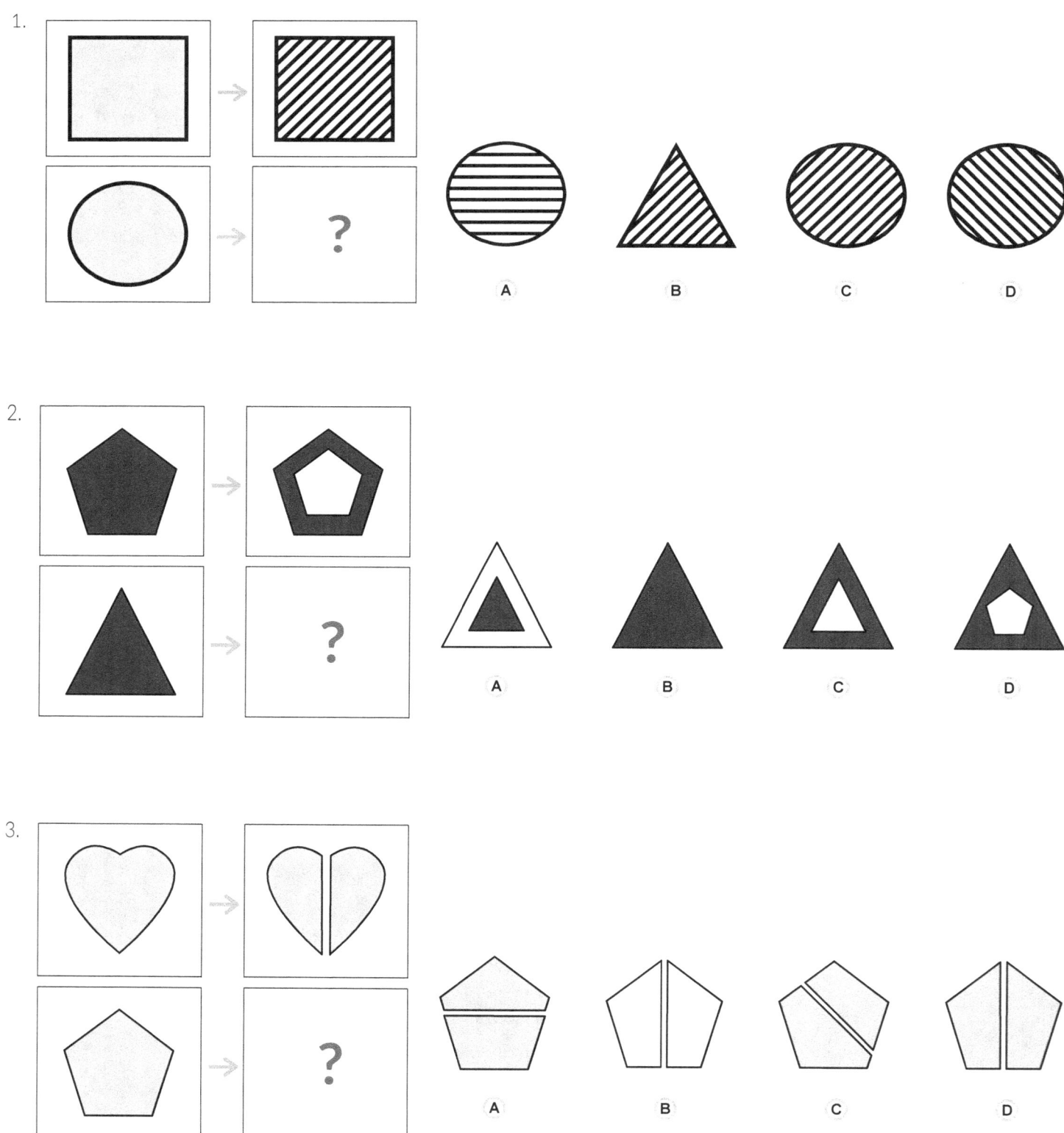

4.

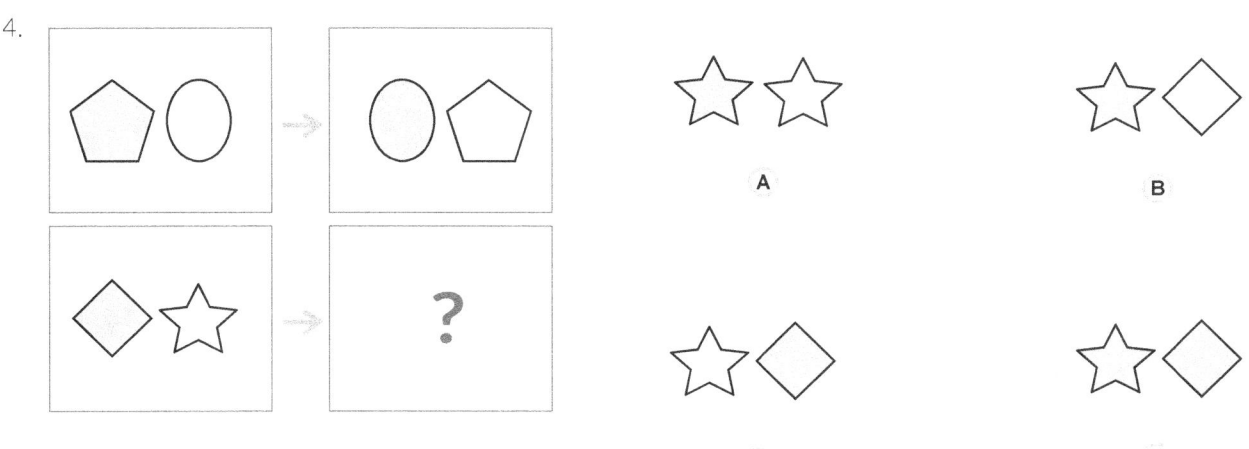

5.

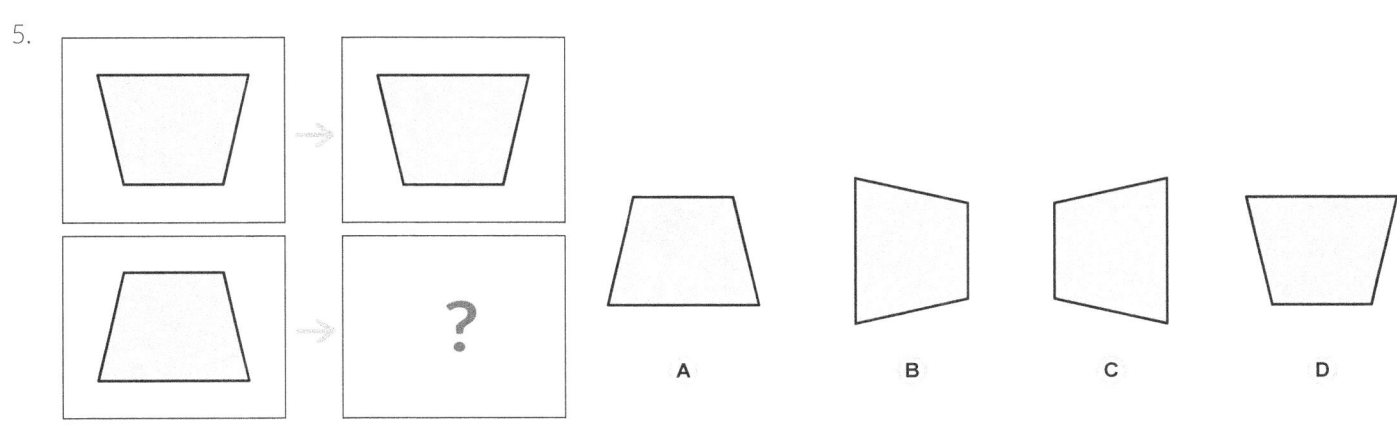

6.

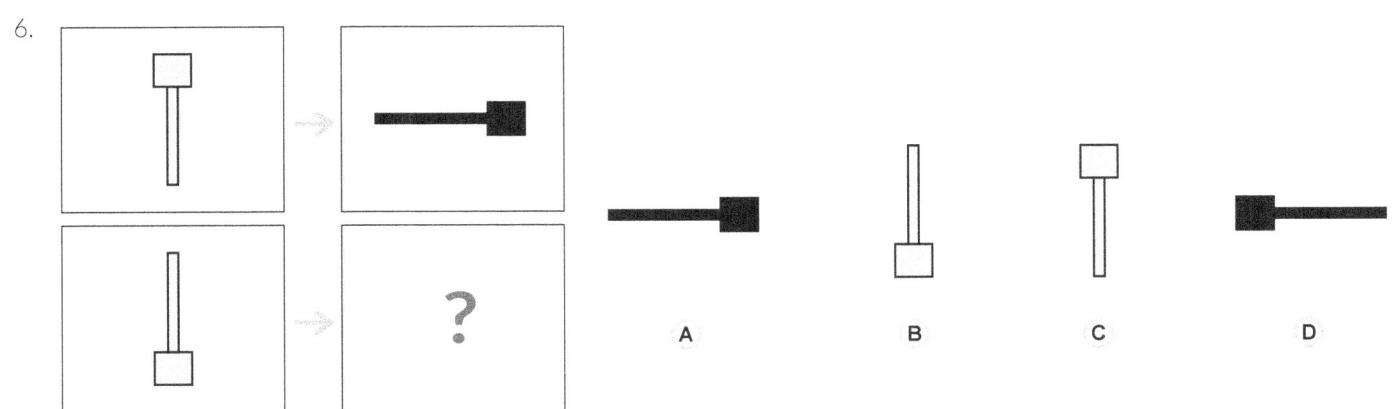

7.

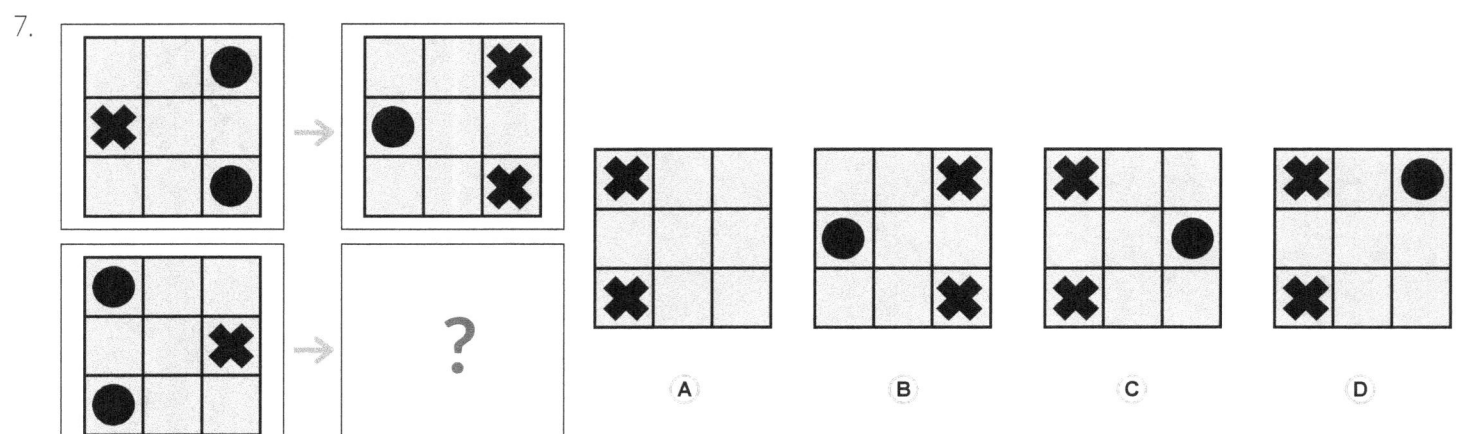

8.

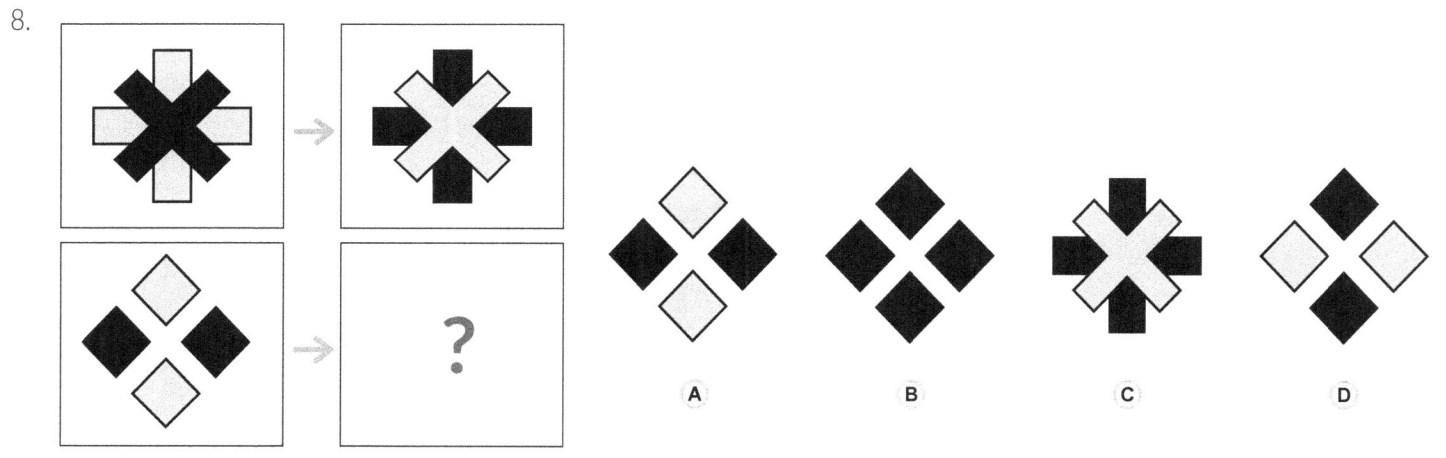

9.

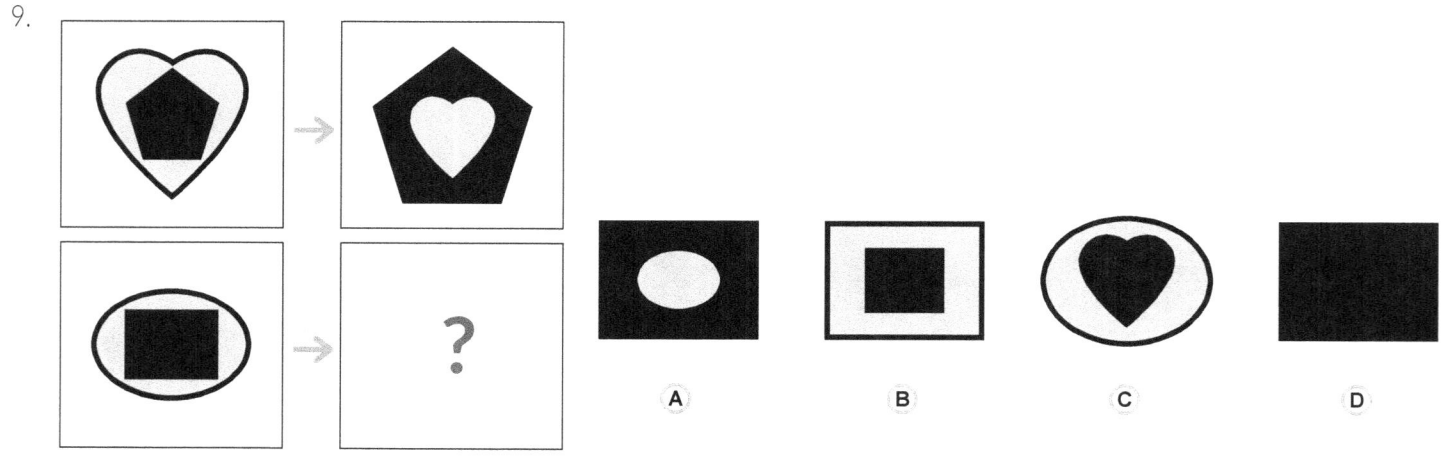

40

10.

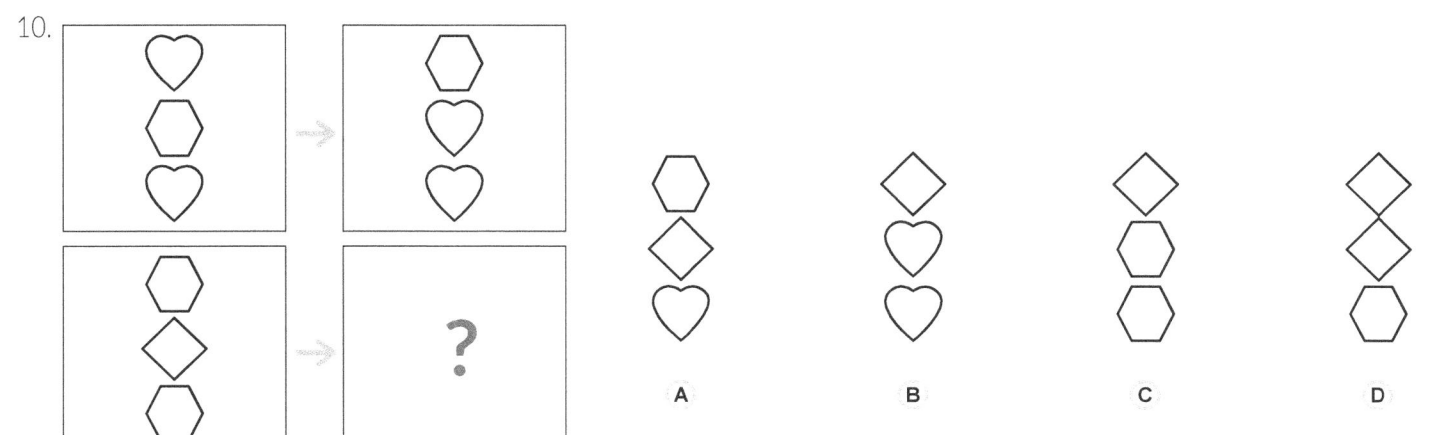

11.

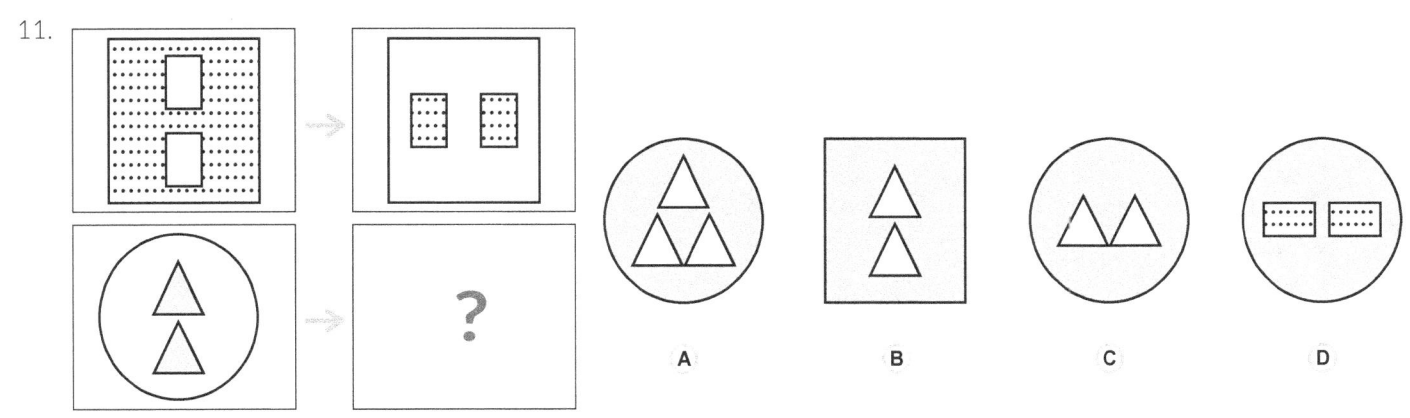

12.

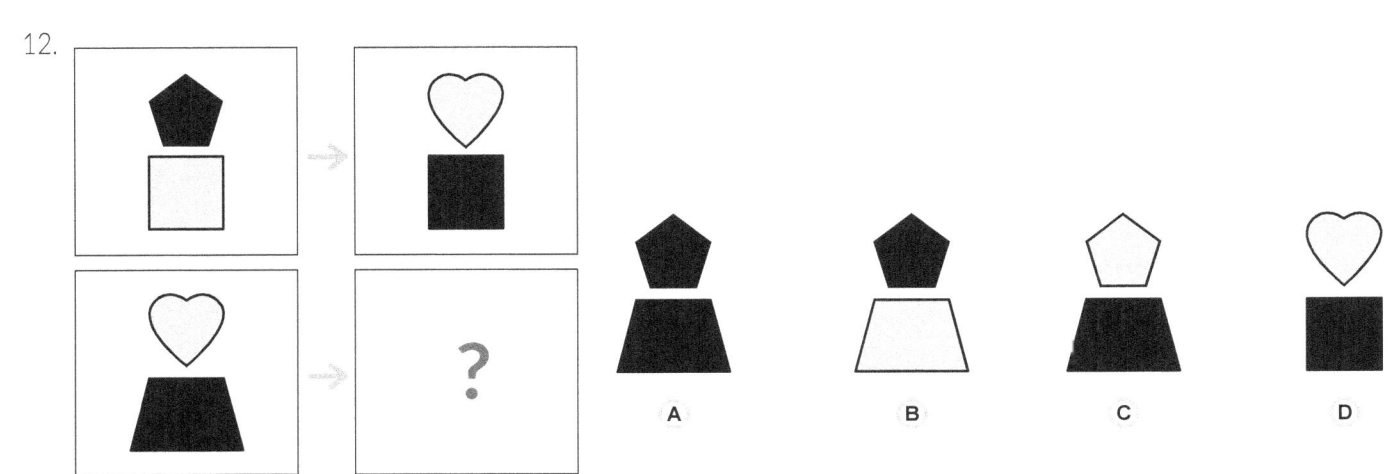

41

13.

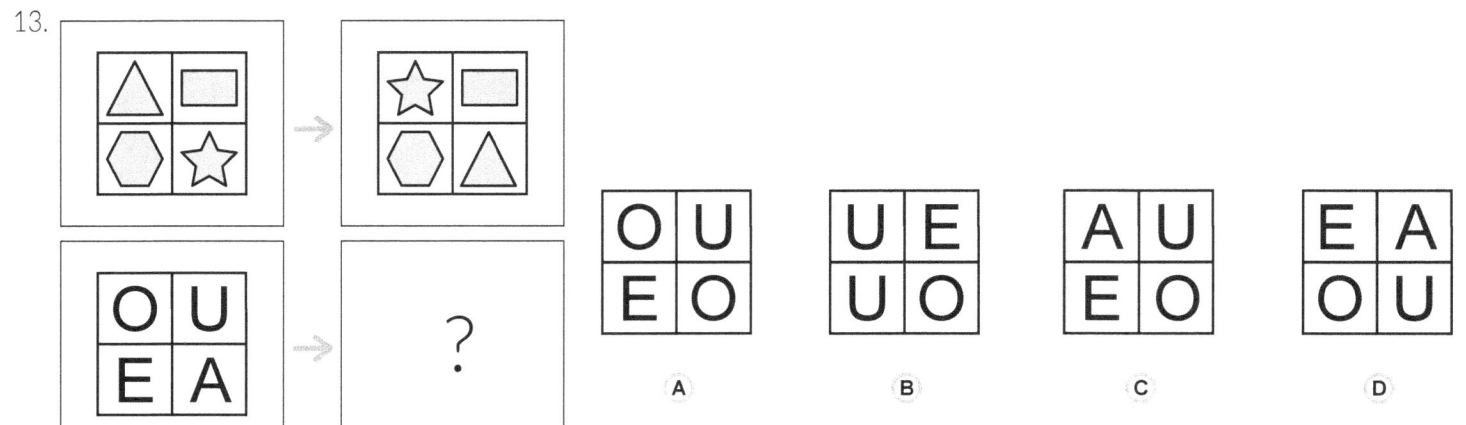

14.

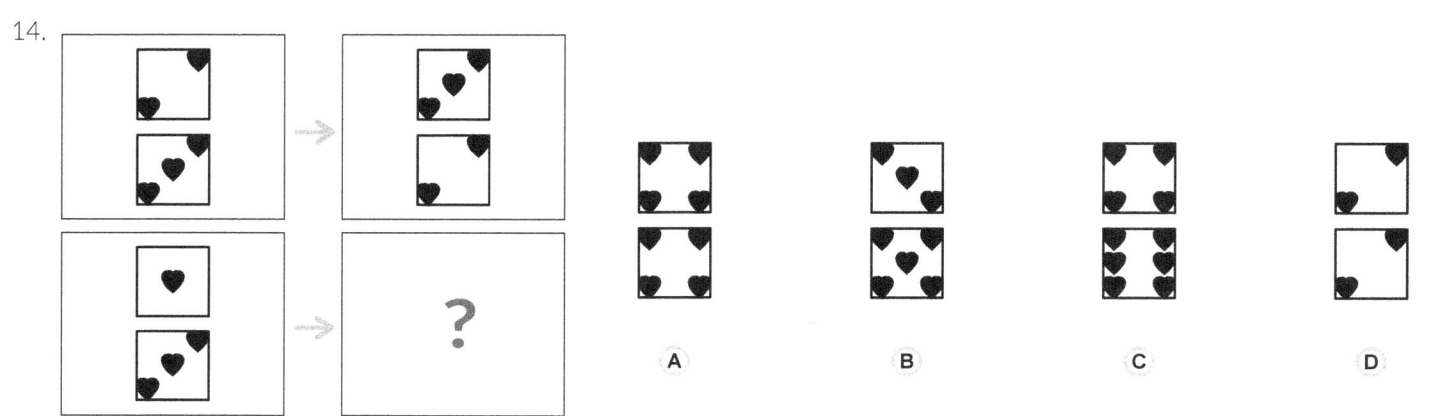

15.

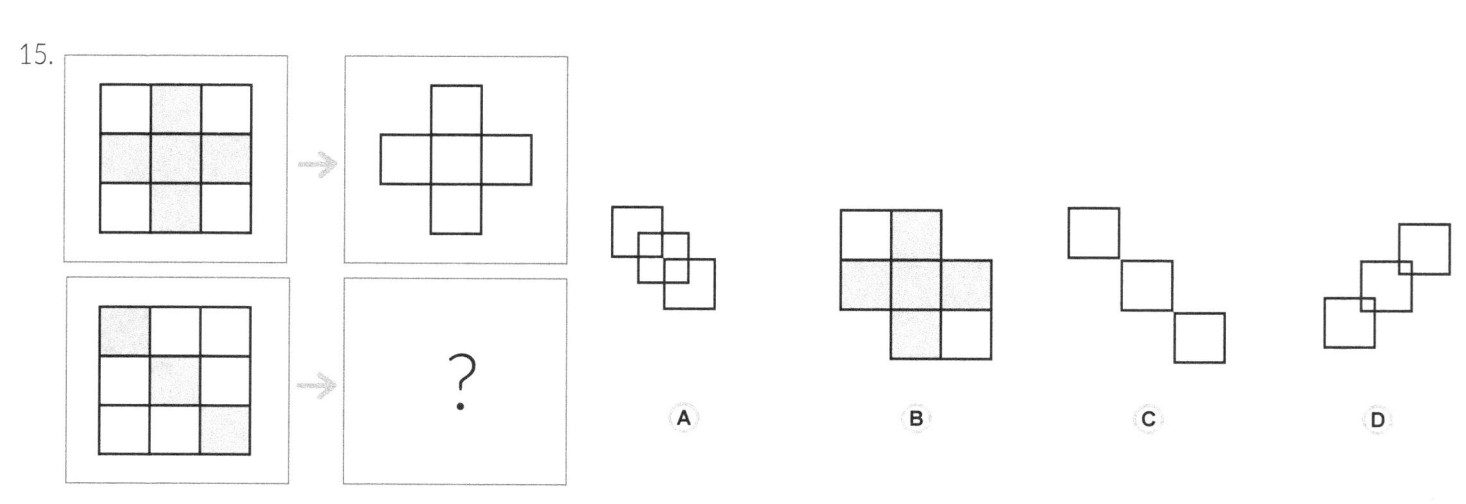

16.

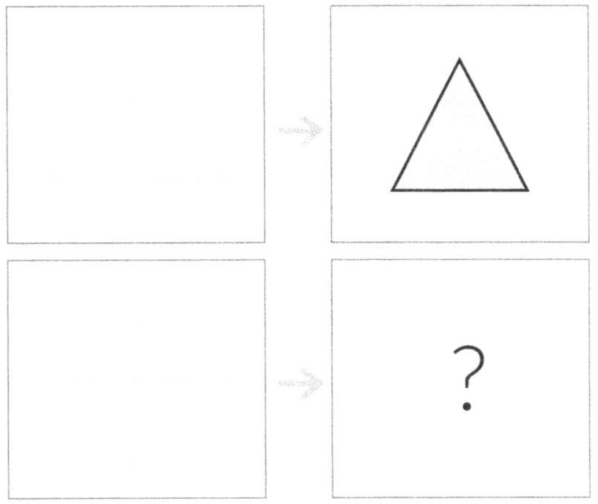

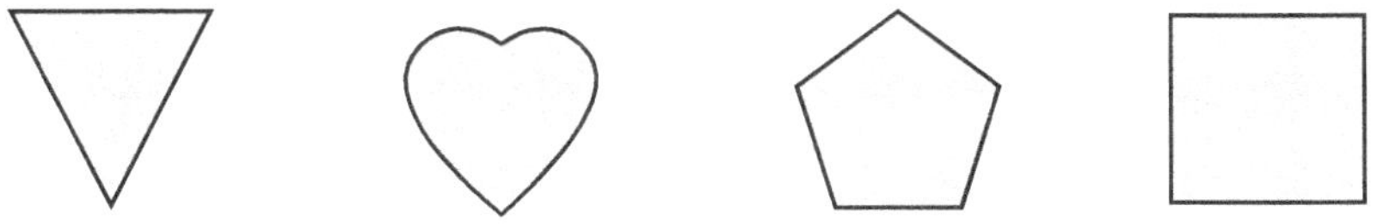

A   B   C   D

17.

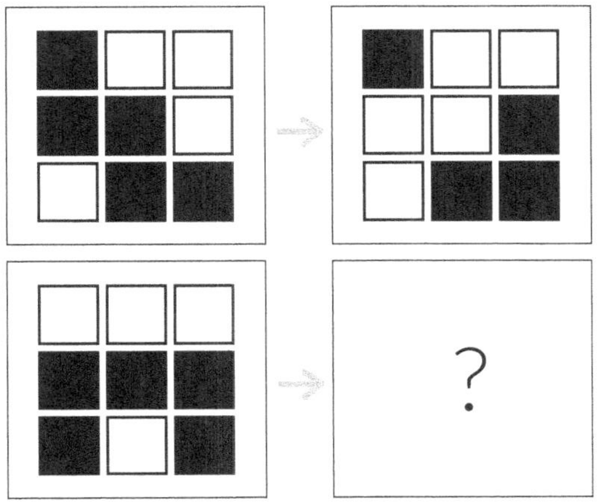

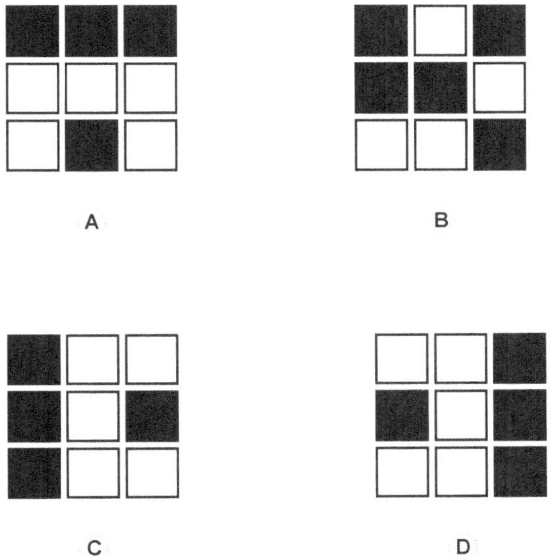

A   B

C   D

Good job!
Let's do some
more!

Caleb

FIGURE CLASSIFICATION

Directions: The top row shows three pictures that are alike in some way. Look at the bottom row. Which bottom picture goes best with the top pictures?

1.

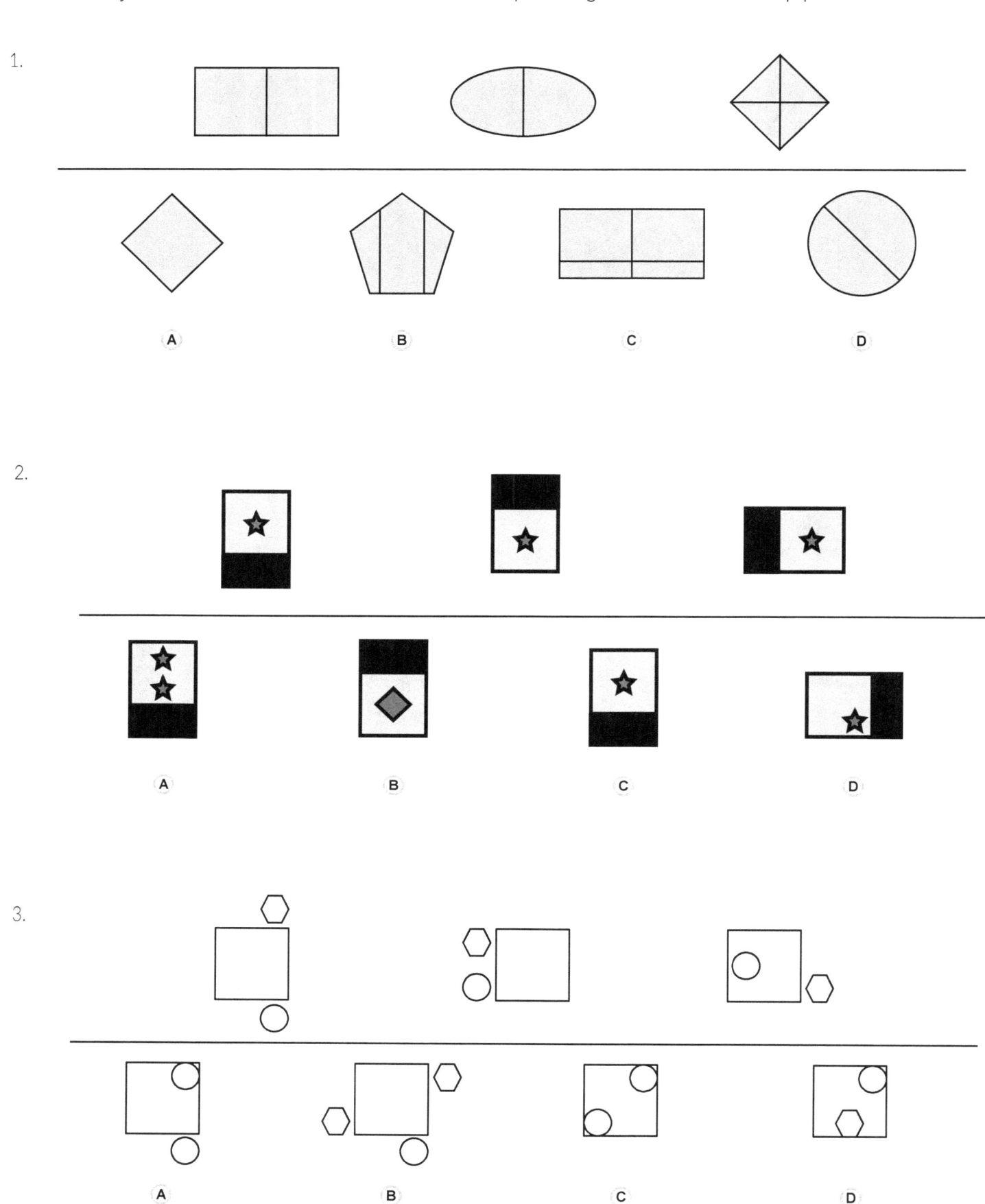

A   B   C   D

2.

A   B   C   D

3.

A   B   C   D

  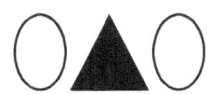

 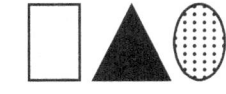 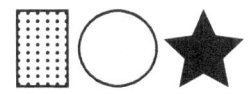 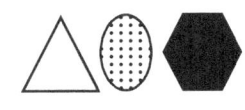

A   B   C   D

5.

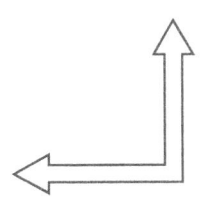 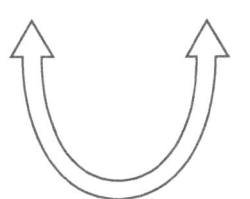 

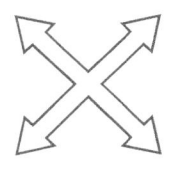 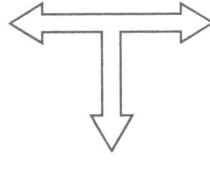  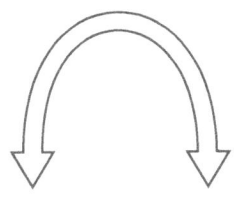

A   B   C   D

6.

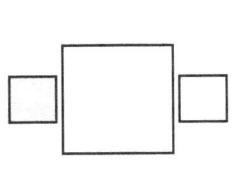 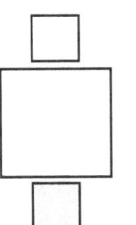 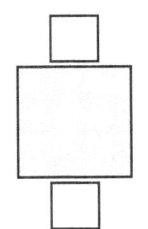

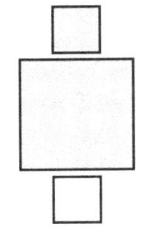 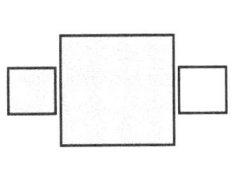 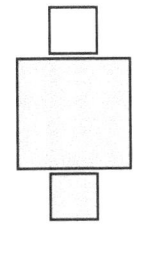 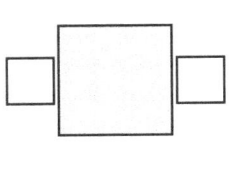

A   B   C   D

7.

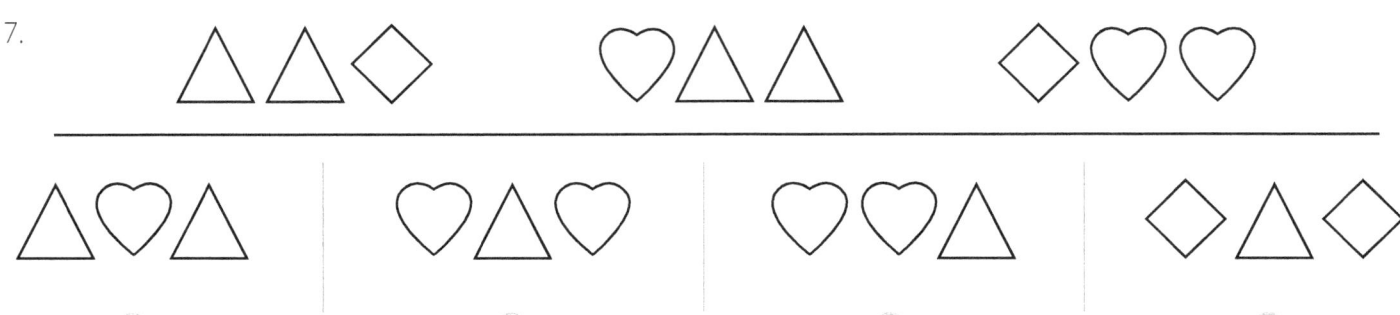

A   B   C   D

8.

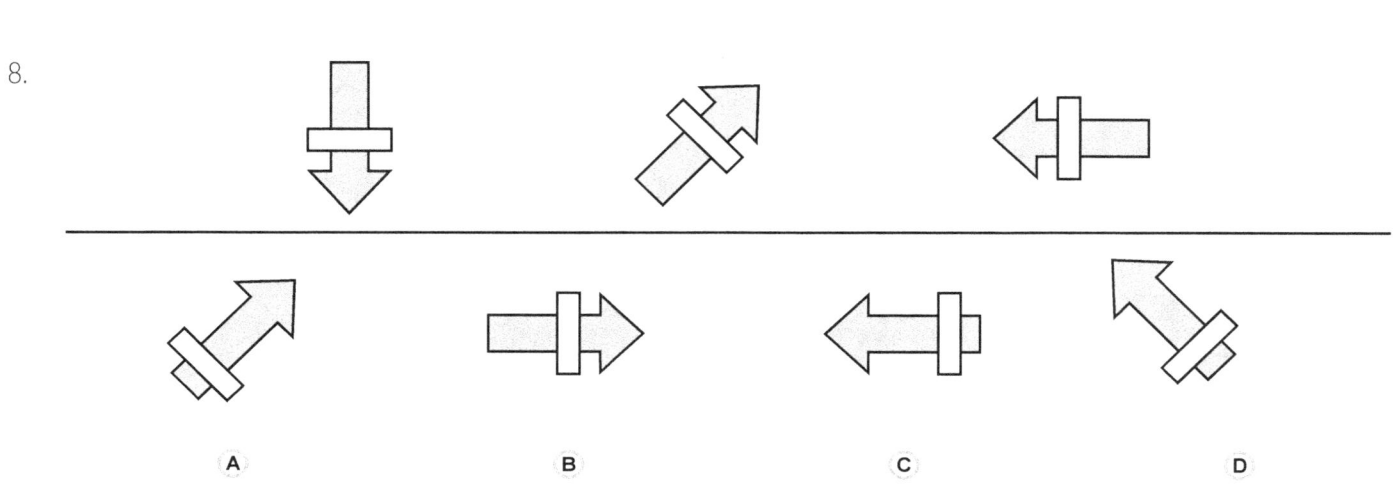

A   B   C   D

9.

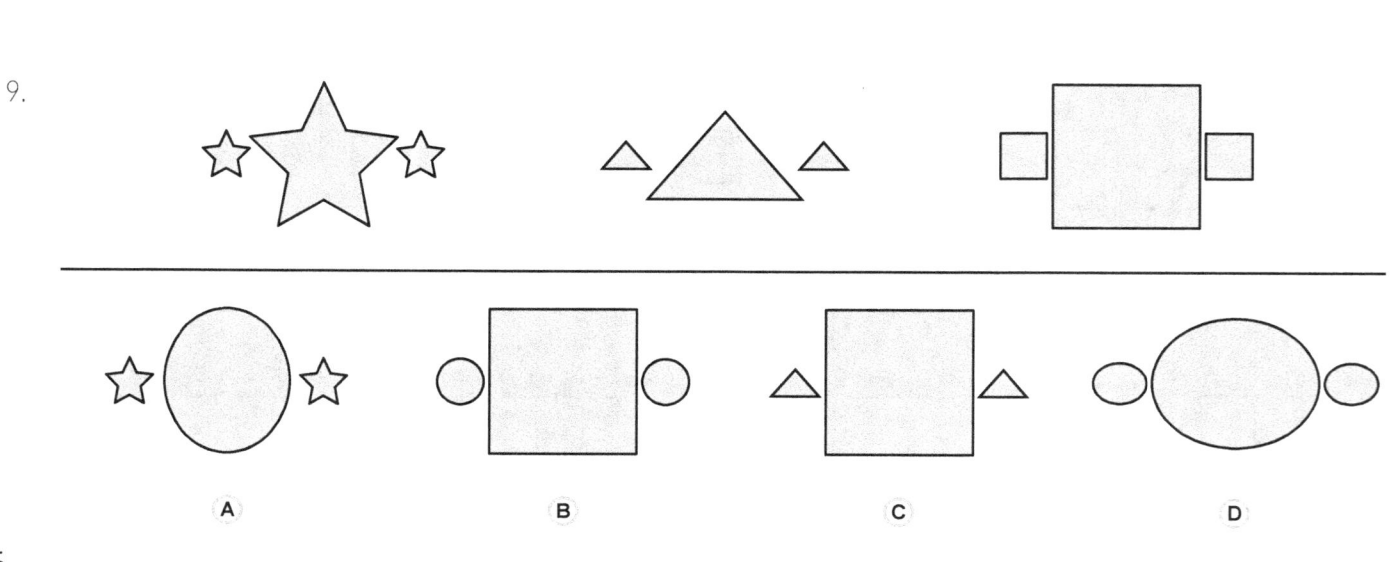

A   B   C   D

10.

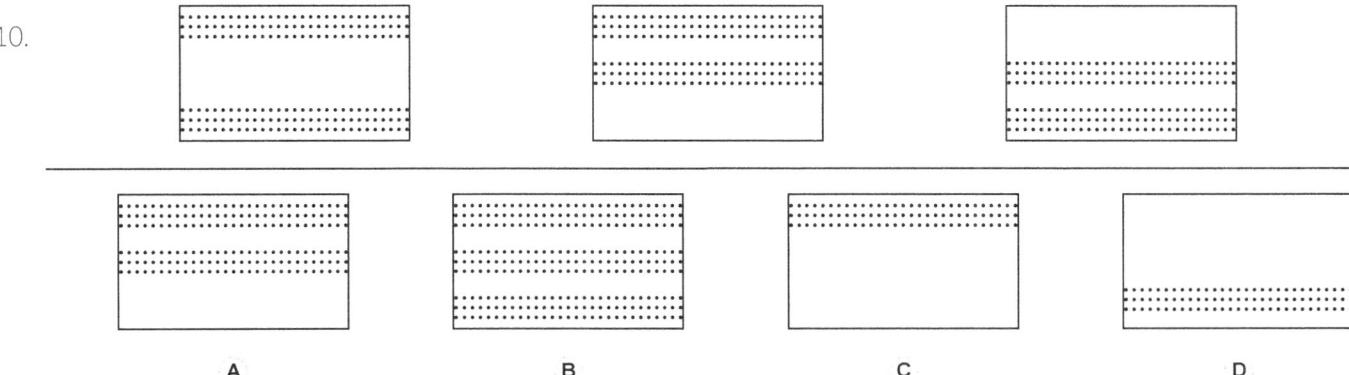

      A   B   C   D

11.

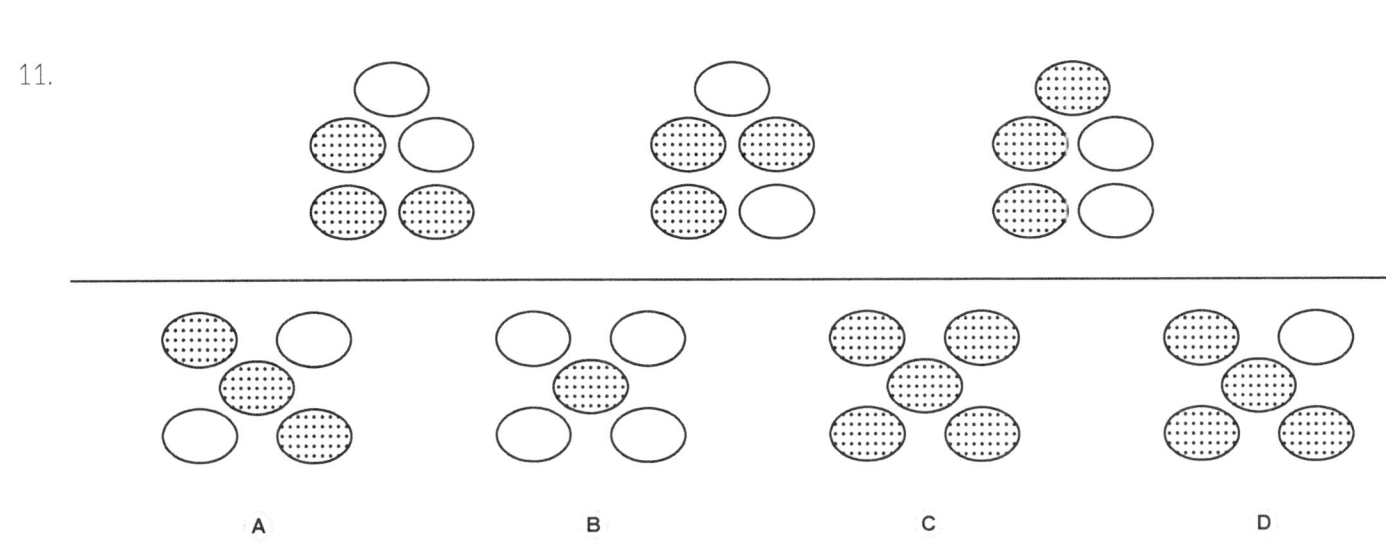

      A   B   C   D

12.

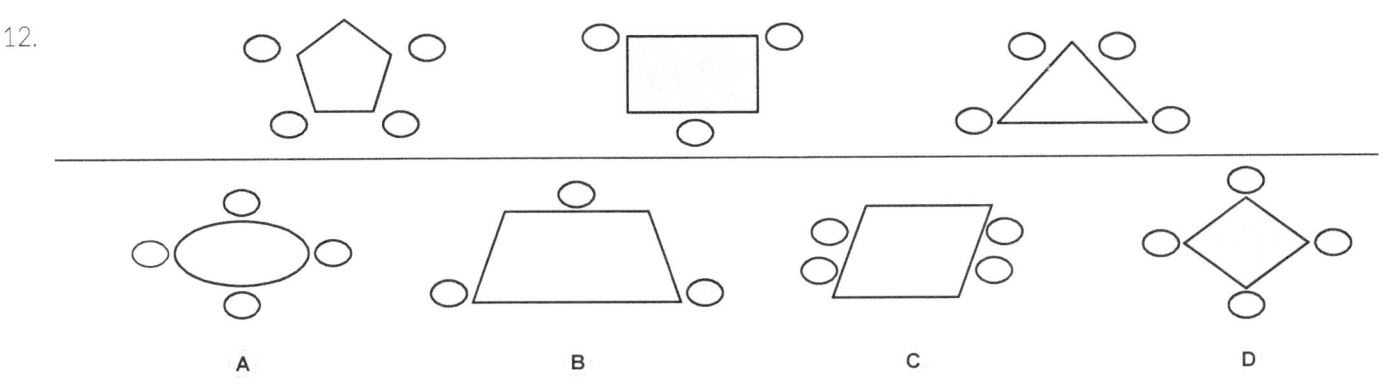

      A   B   C   D

13.

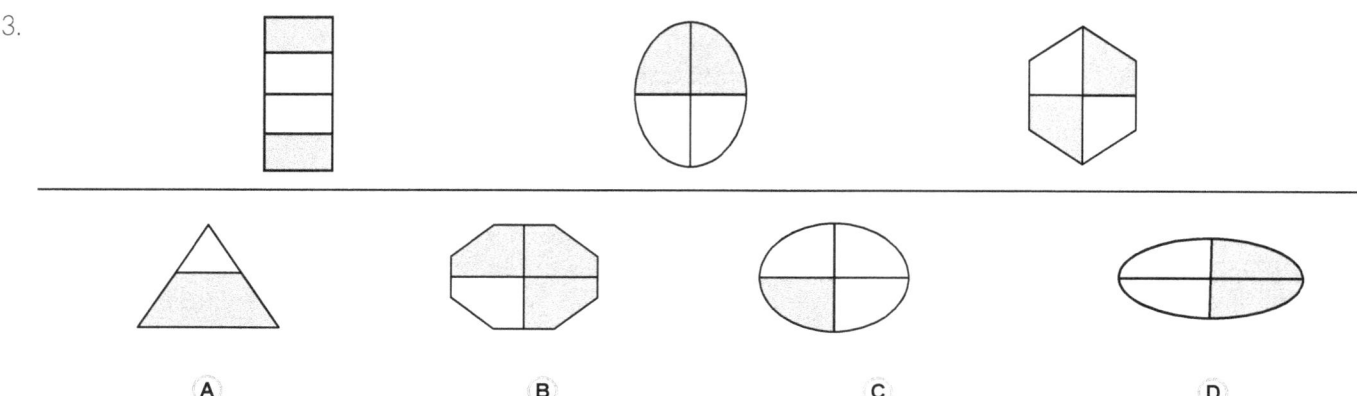

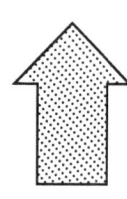

(A)

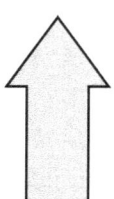

(B)

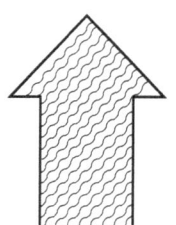

(C)

(D)

14.

(A)

(B)

(C)

(D)

15.

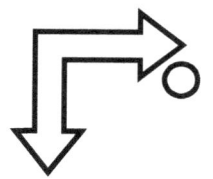

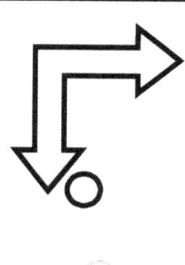

(A)

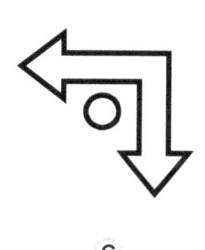

(B)

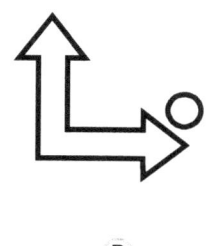

(C)

(D)

48

PAPER FOLDING

The top row of pictures shows a sheet of paper. The paper was folded, then something was cut out.
Which picture in the bottom row shows how the paper would look after it's unfolded?

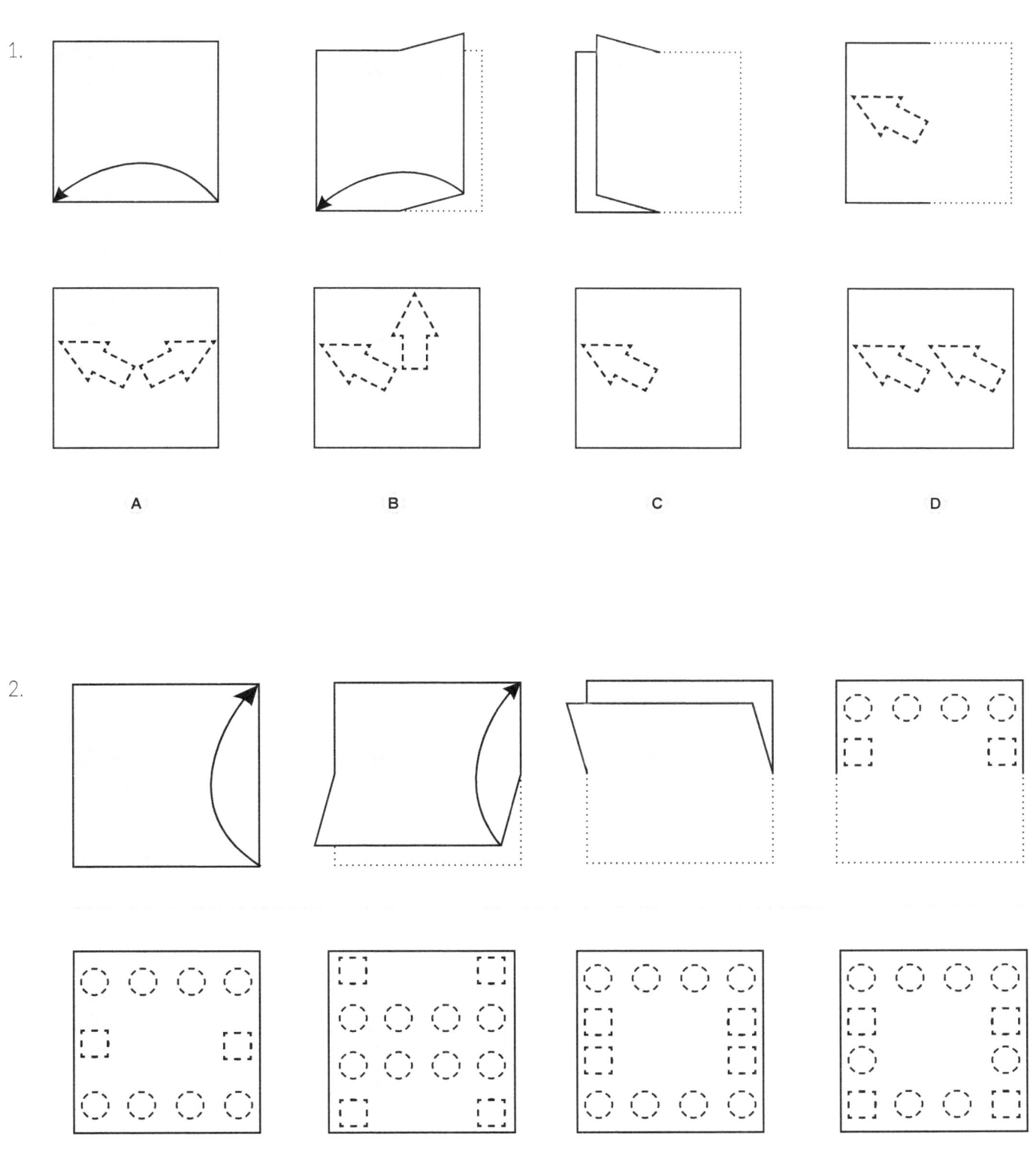

3.

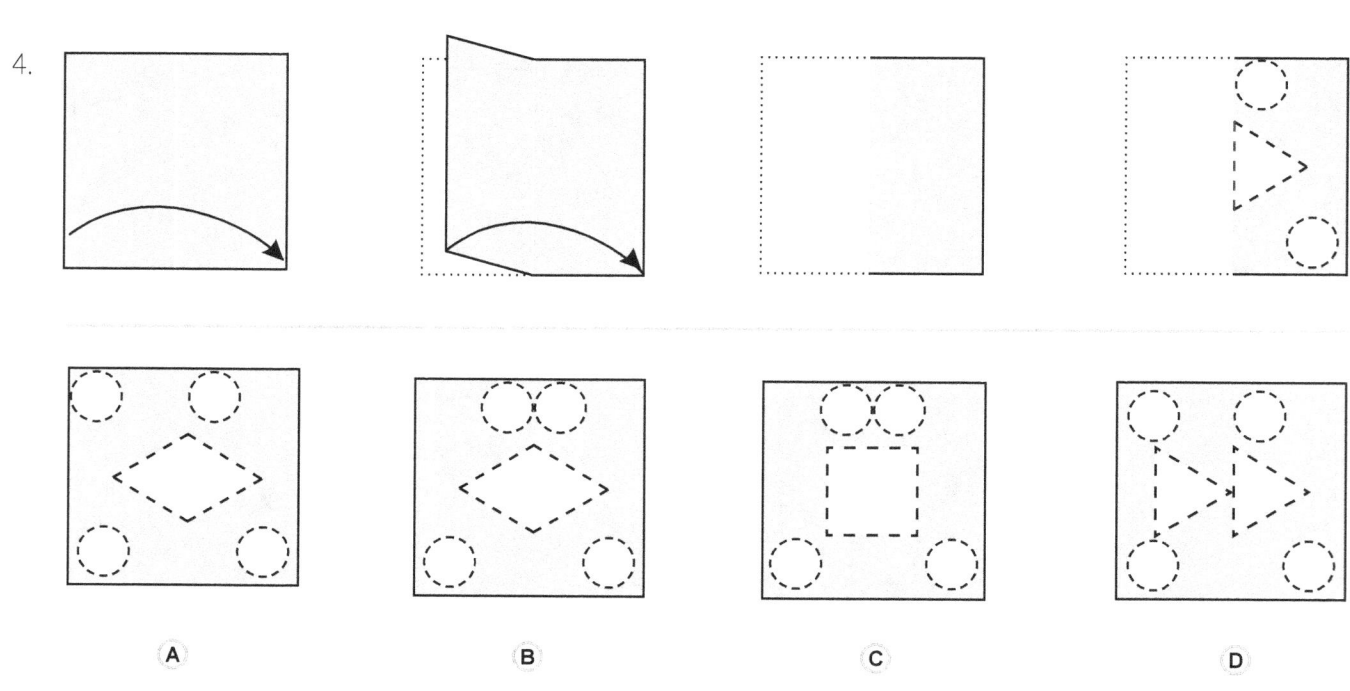

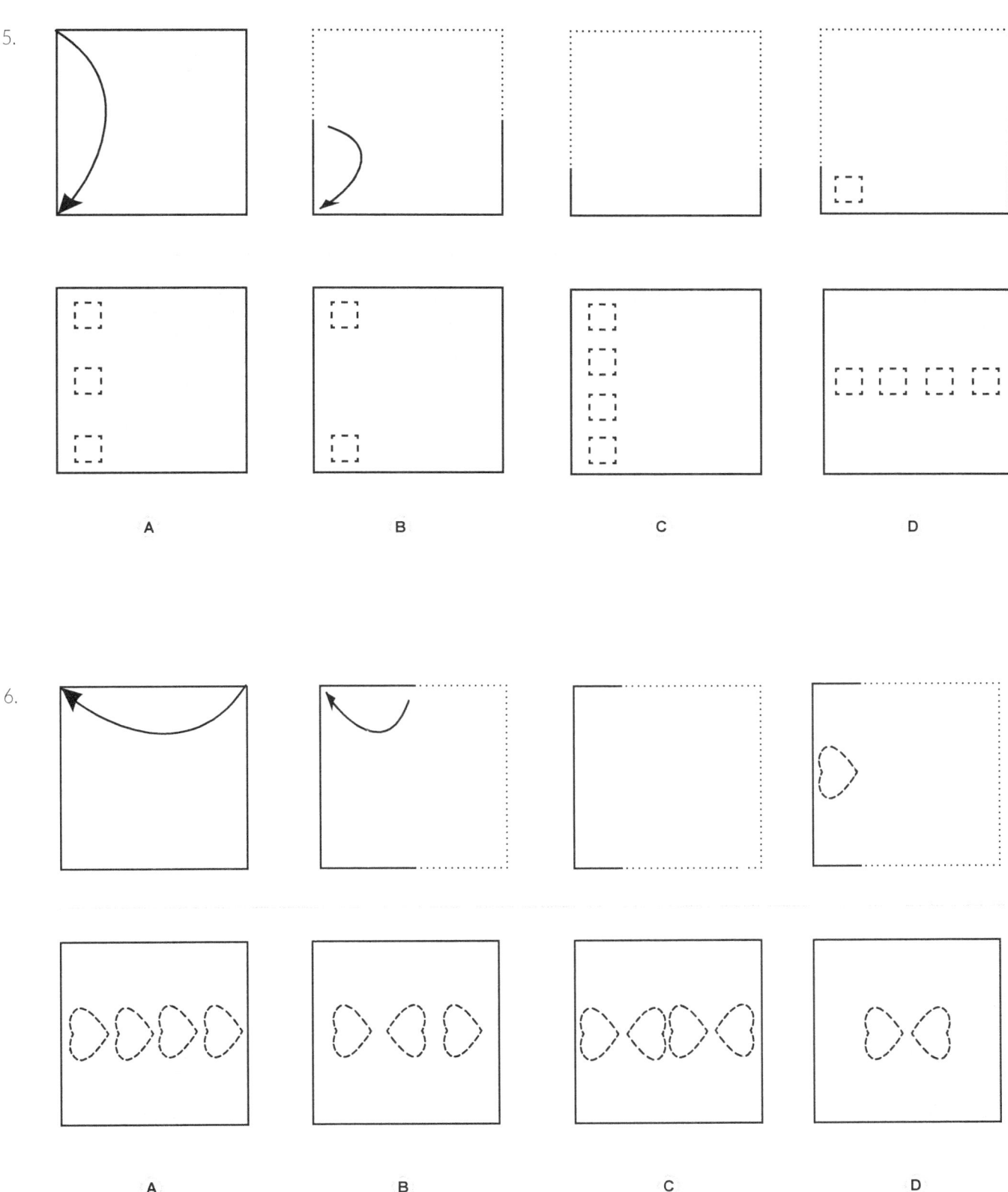

5.

A   B   C   D

6.

A   B   C   D

7.

A   B   C   D

8.

A   B   C   D

9.

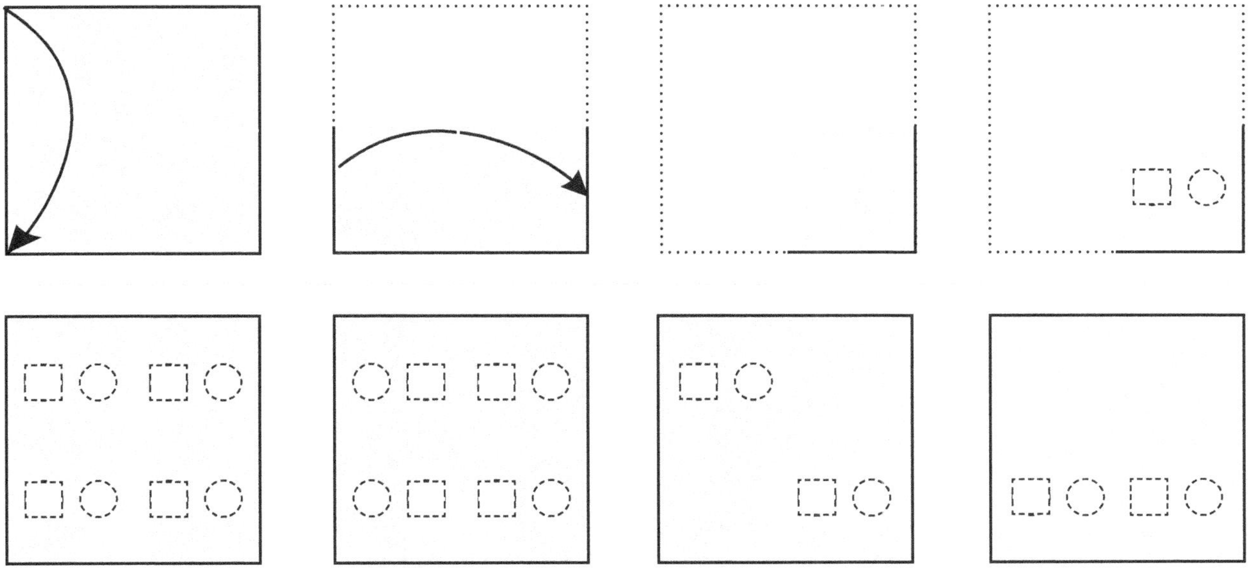

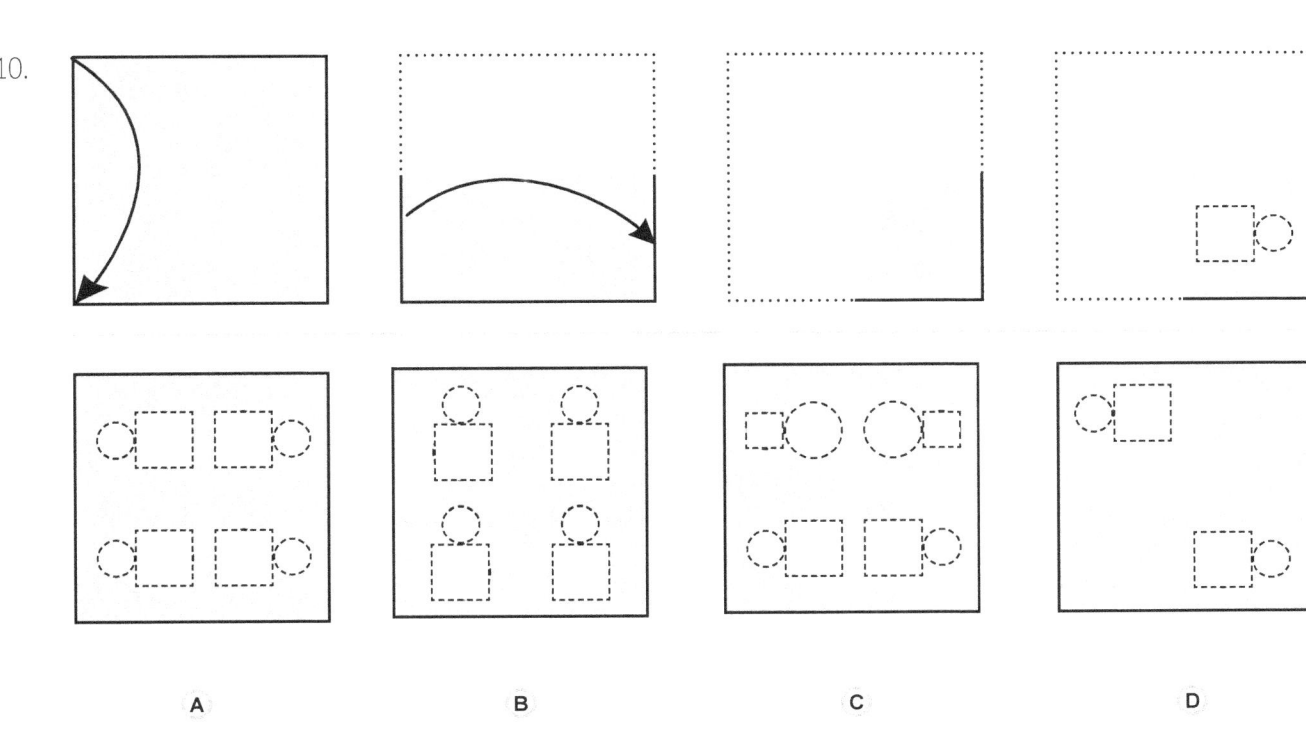

A   B   C   D

10.

A   B   C   D

11.

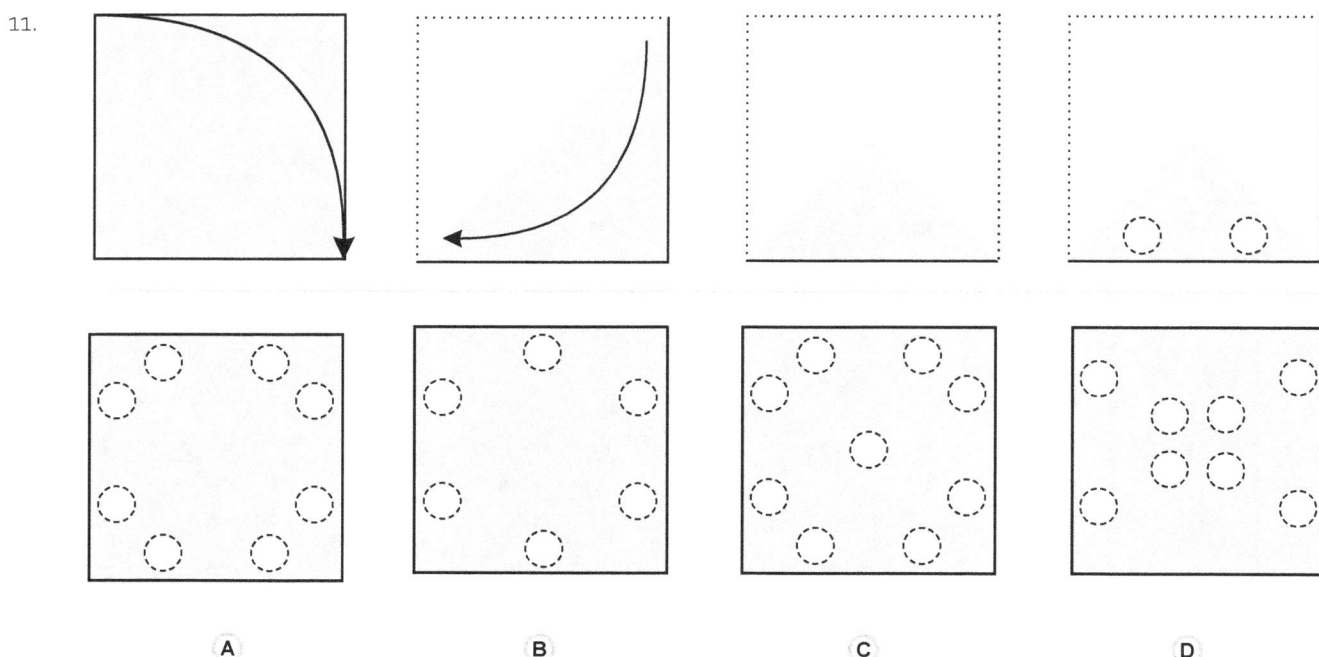

A   B   C   D

12.

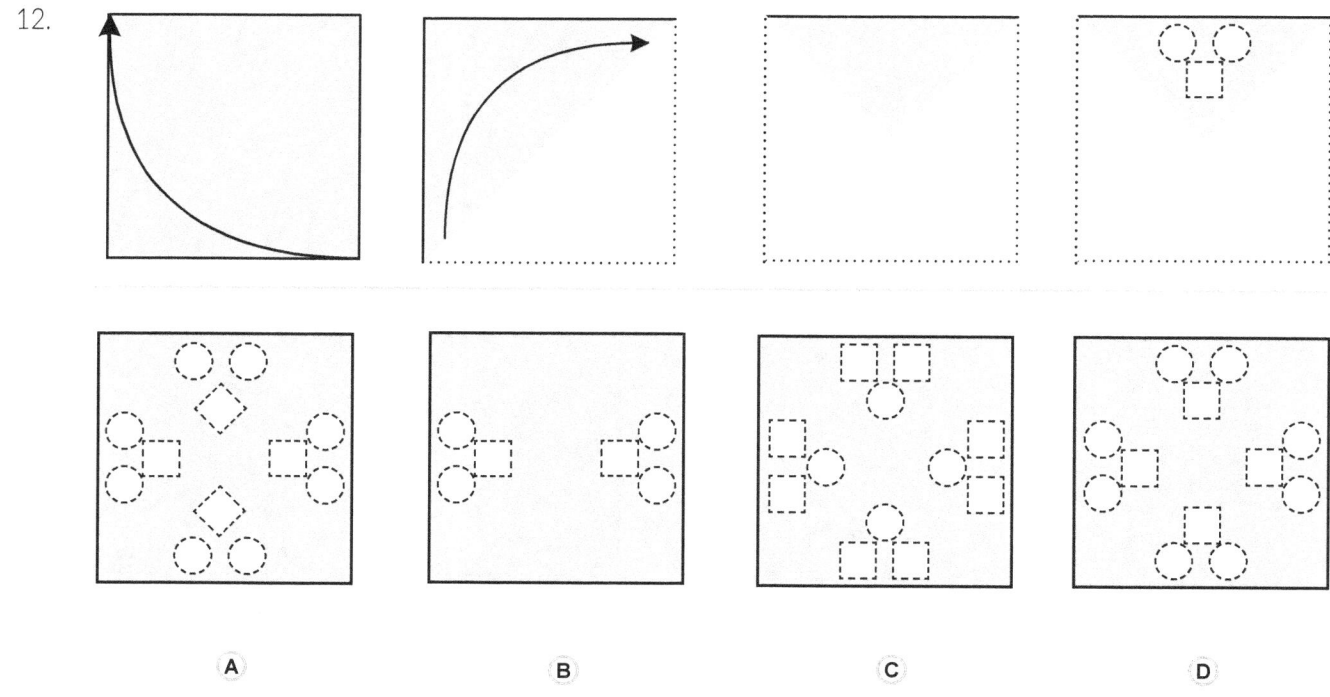

A   B   C   D

13.

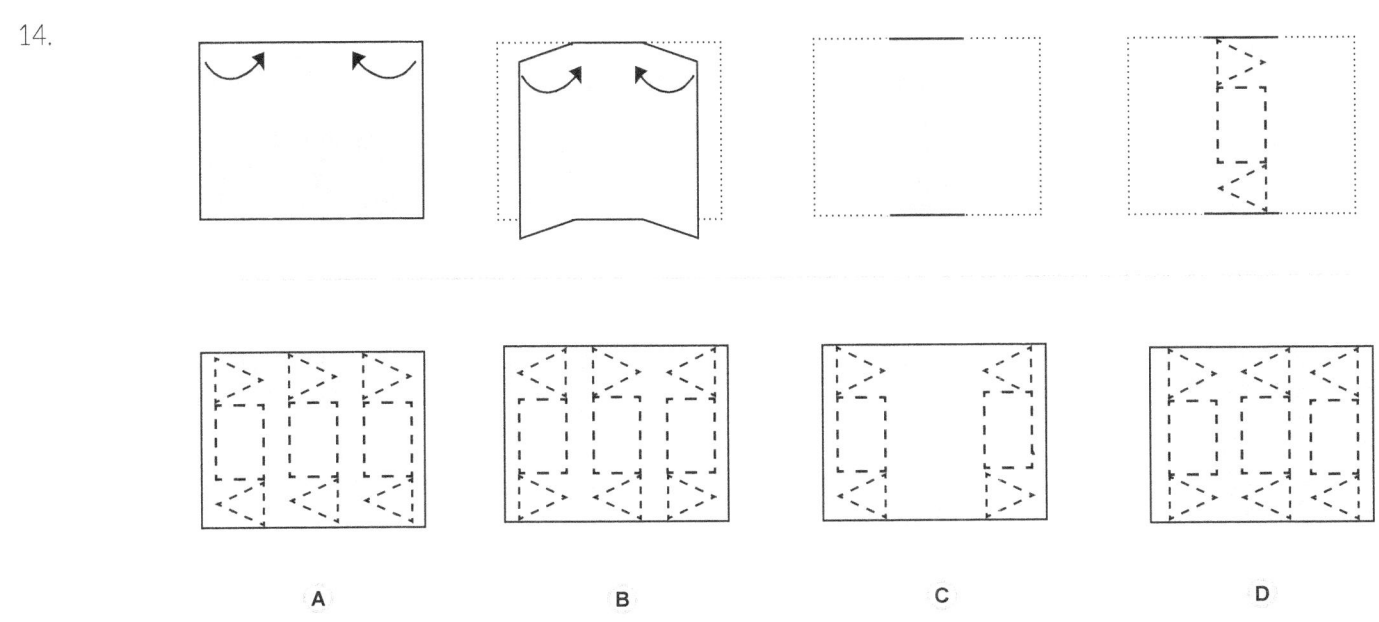

A   B   C   D

14.

A   B   C   D

15.

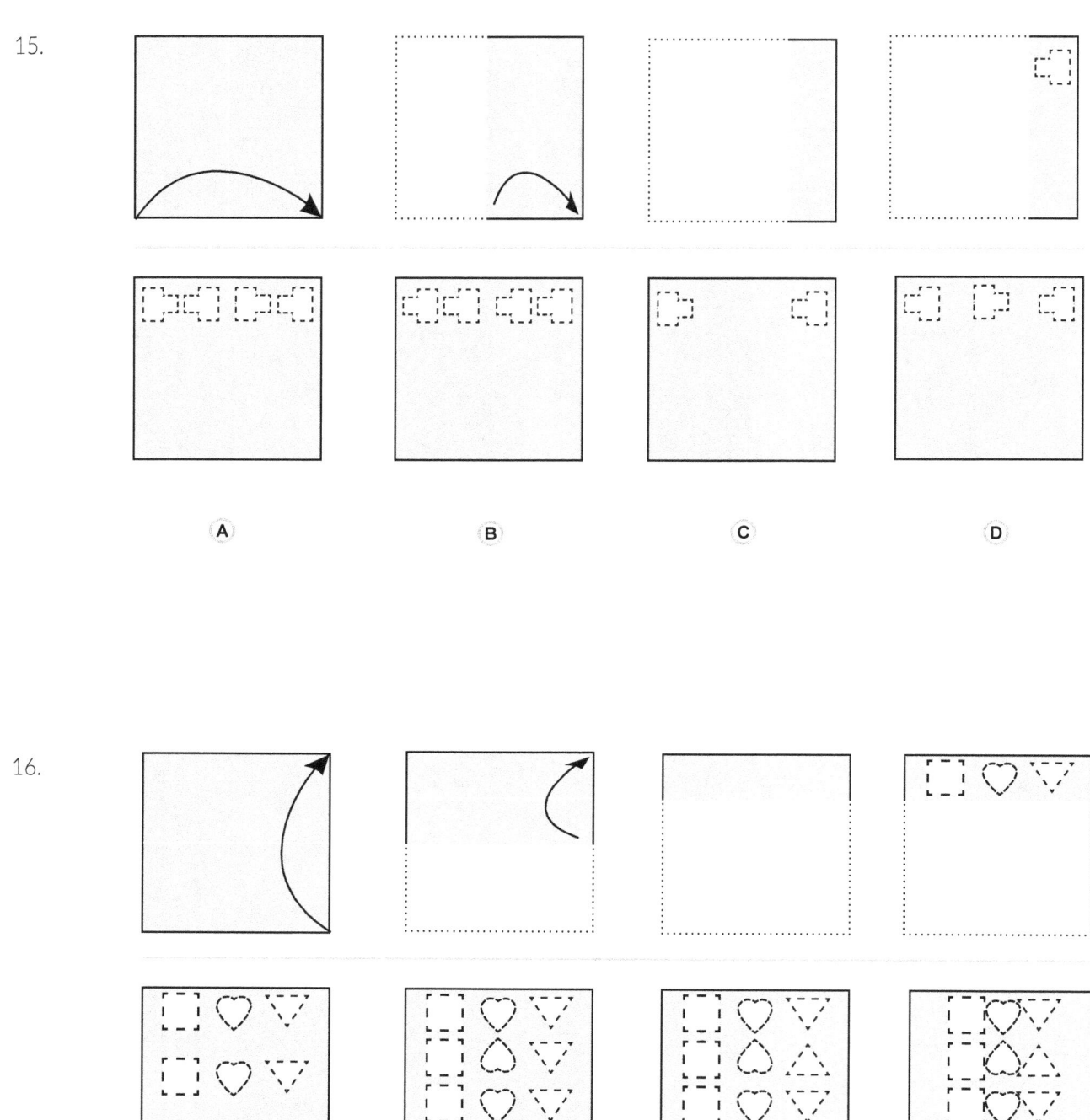

A   B   C   D

16.

A   B   C   D

- End of Practice Test 2 -

COGAT® PRACTICE TEST 3

Directions: The pictures in the top boxes go together in some way. One of the bottom boxes is empty. Which answer choice goes with the picture in the bottom box in the same way the top pictures do?

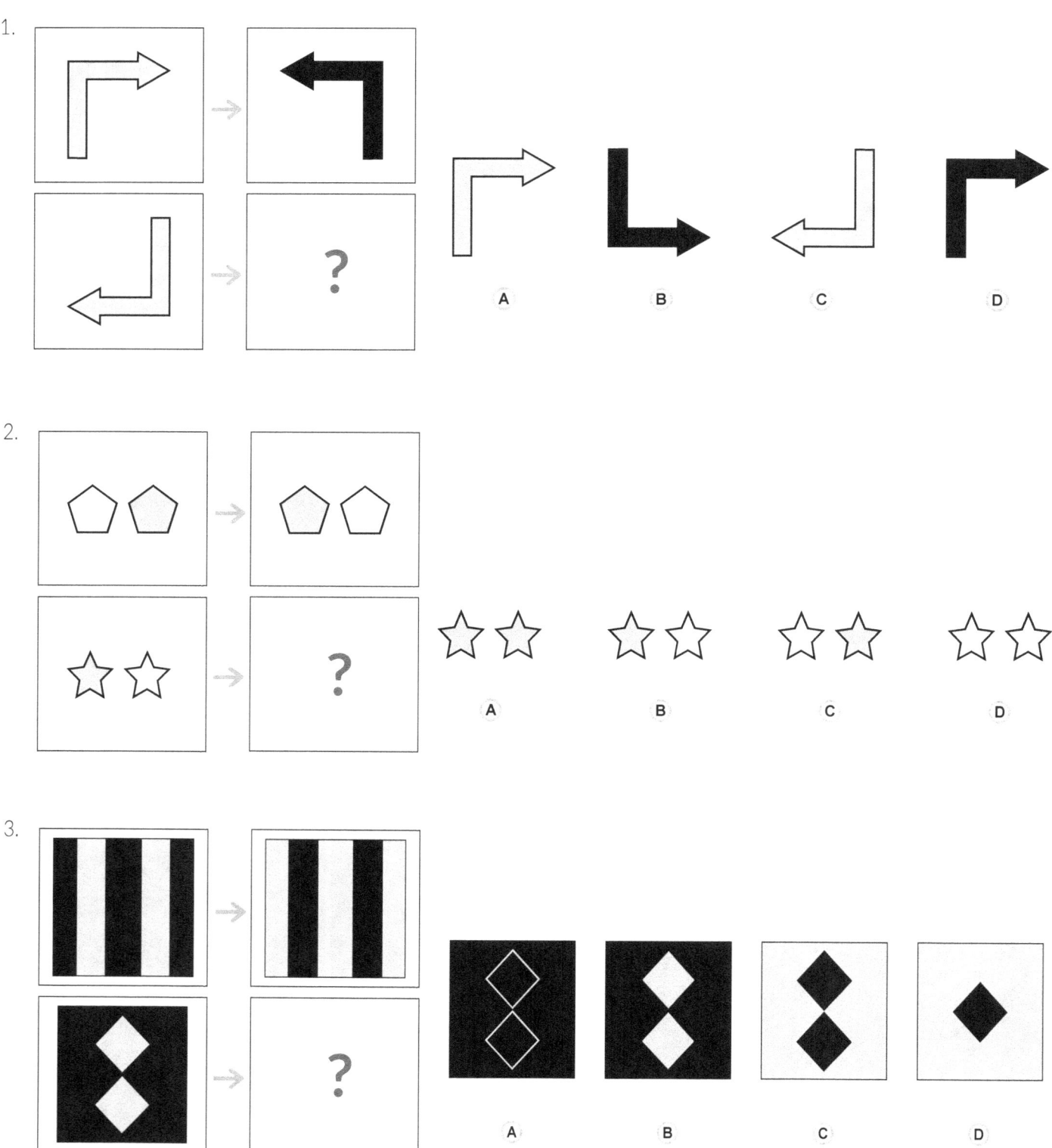

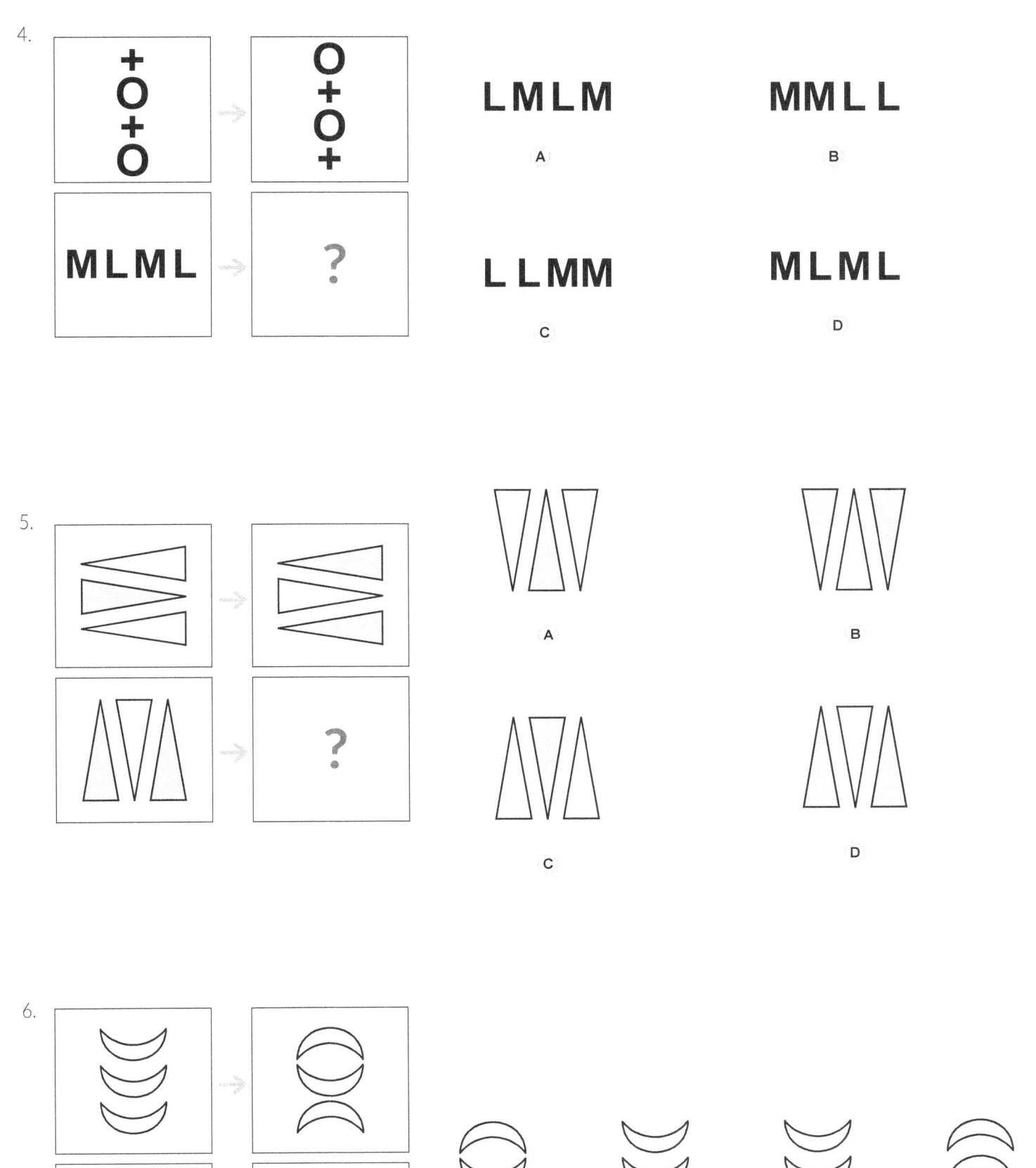

4.

A. LMLM
B. MMLL
C. LLMM
D. MLML

5.

6.

59

7.

 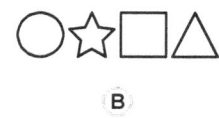

A

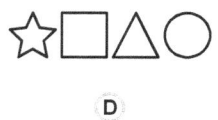

B

C

D

8.

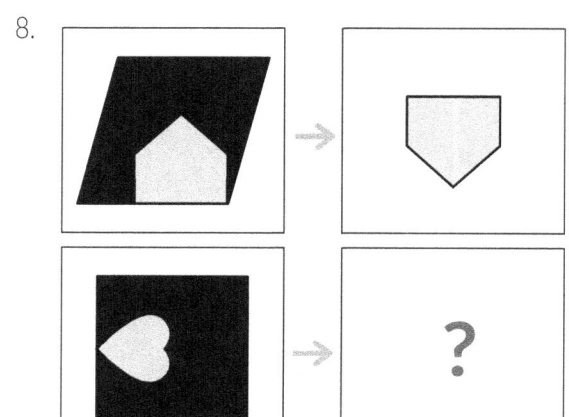

A

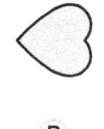
B

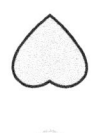
C

D

9.

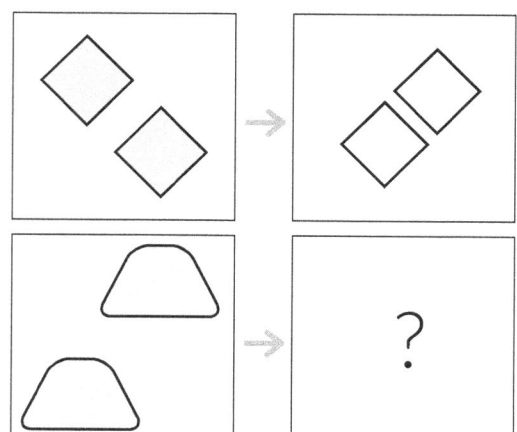

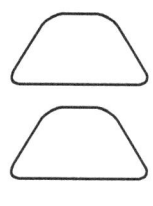
A

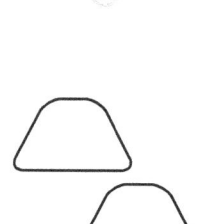
B

C

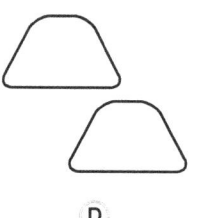
D

10.

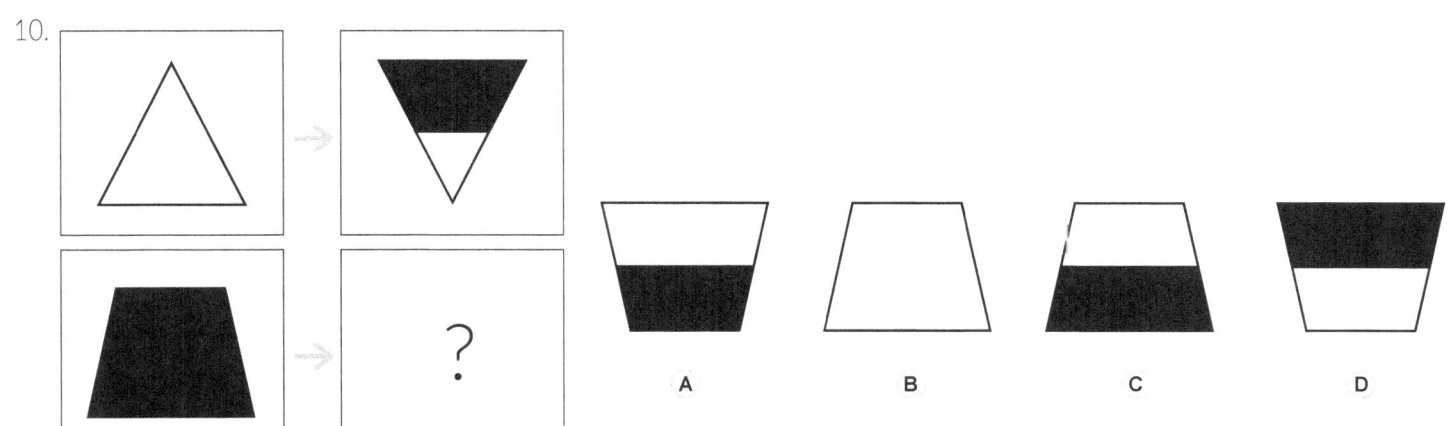

11.

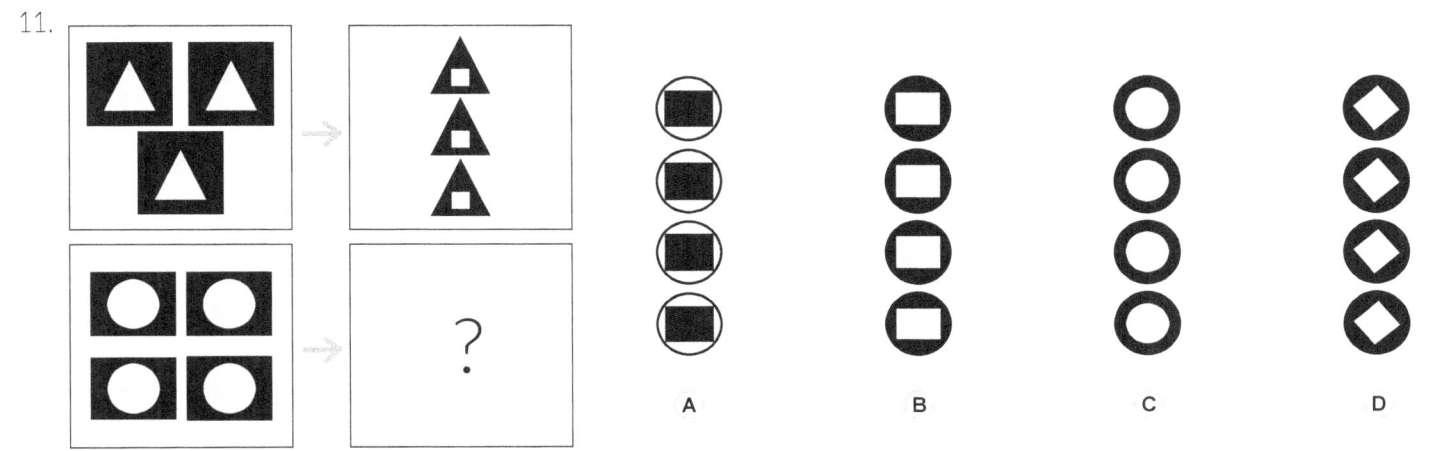

12.

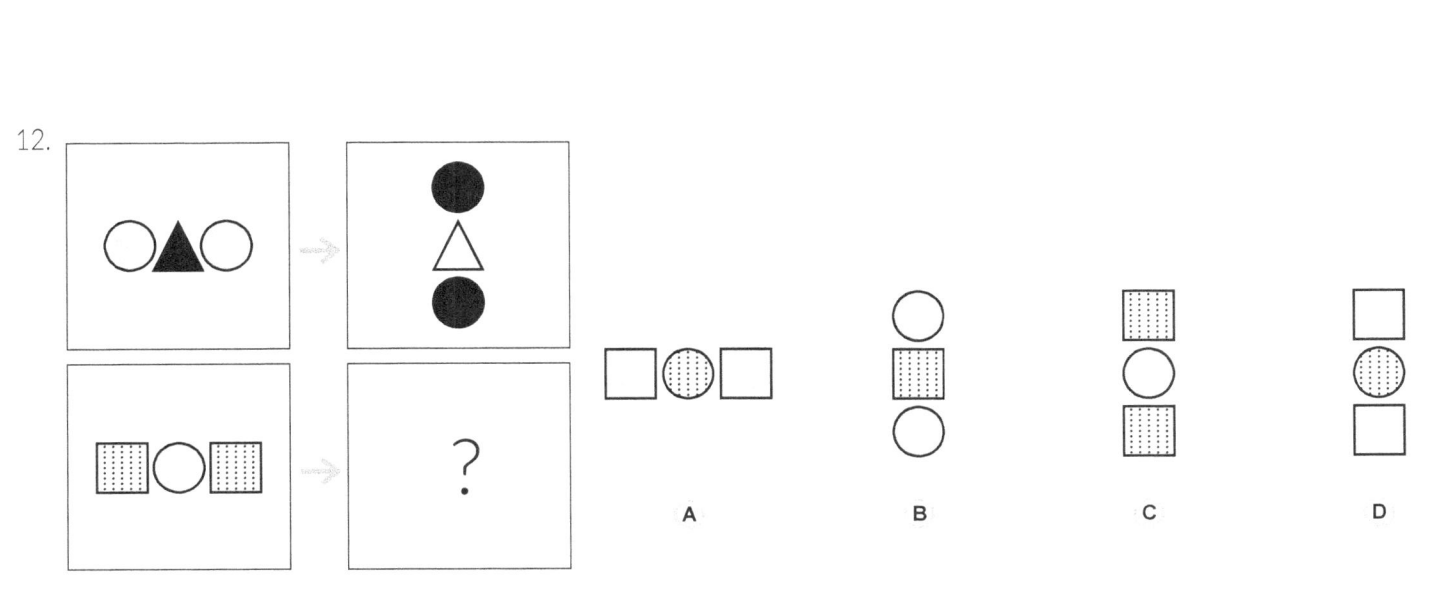

61

13.

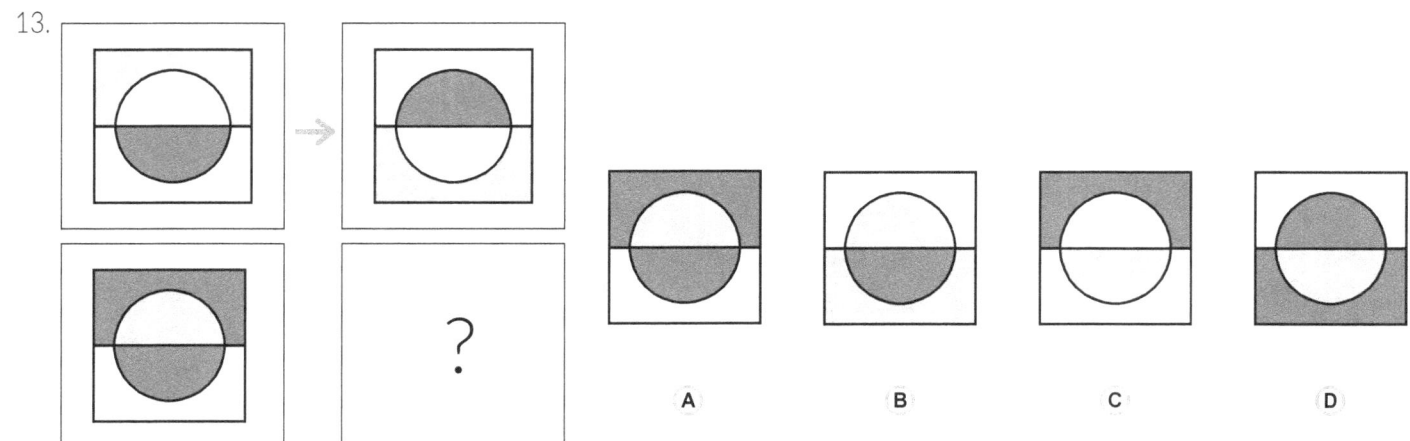

14.

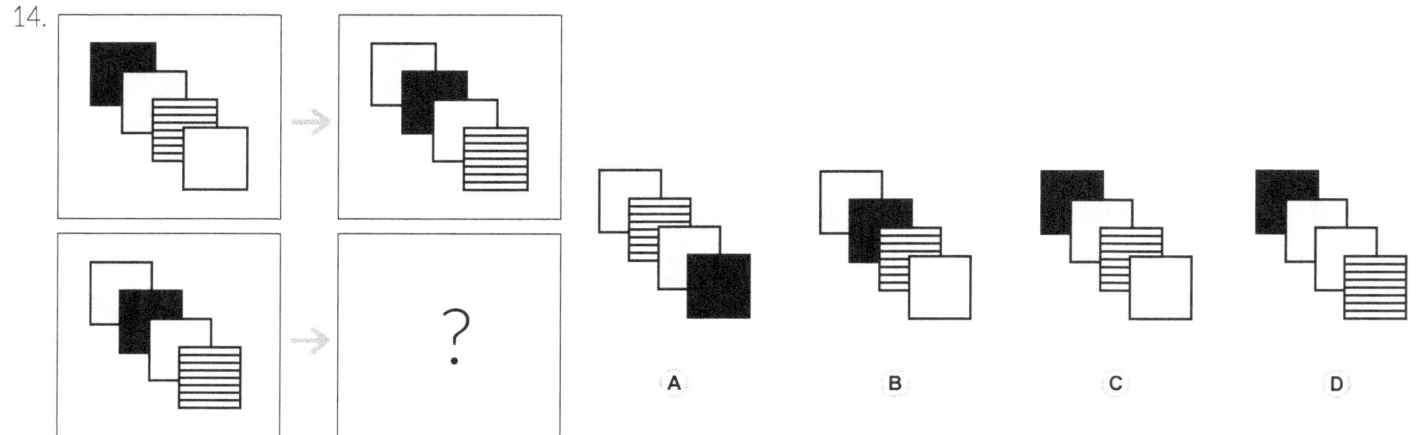

15.

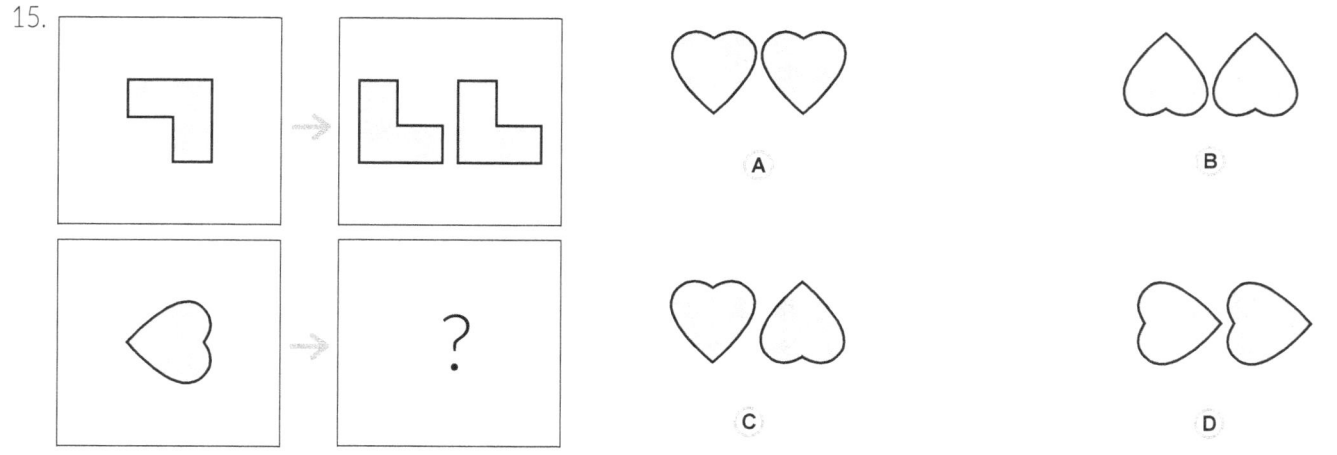

62

16.

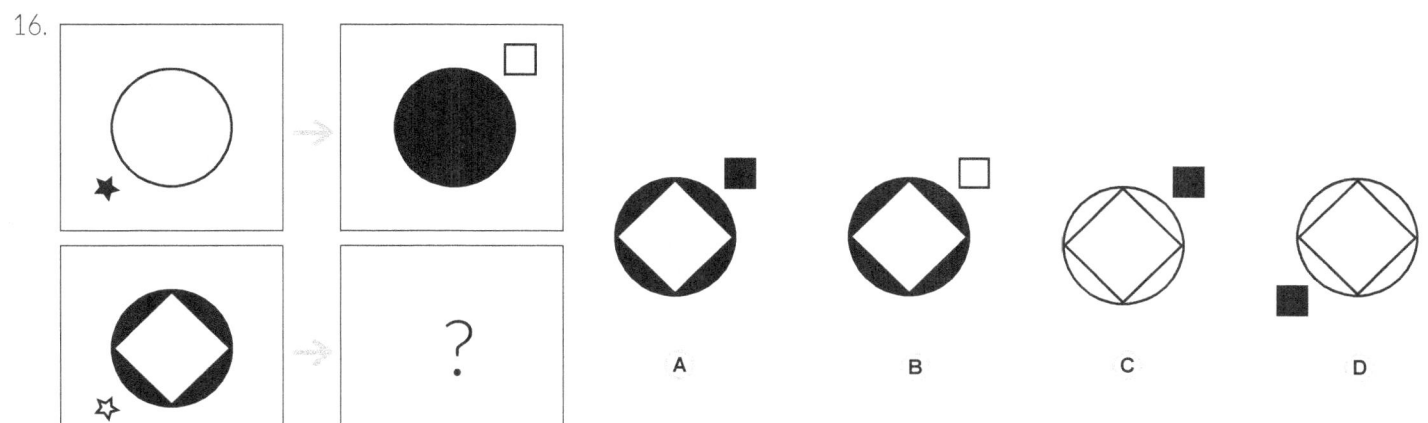

17.

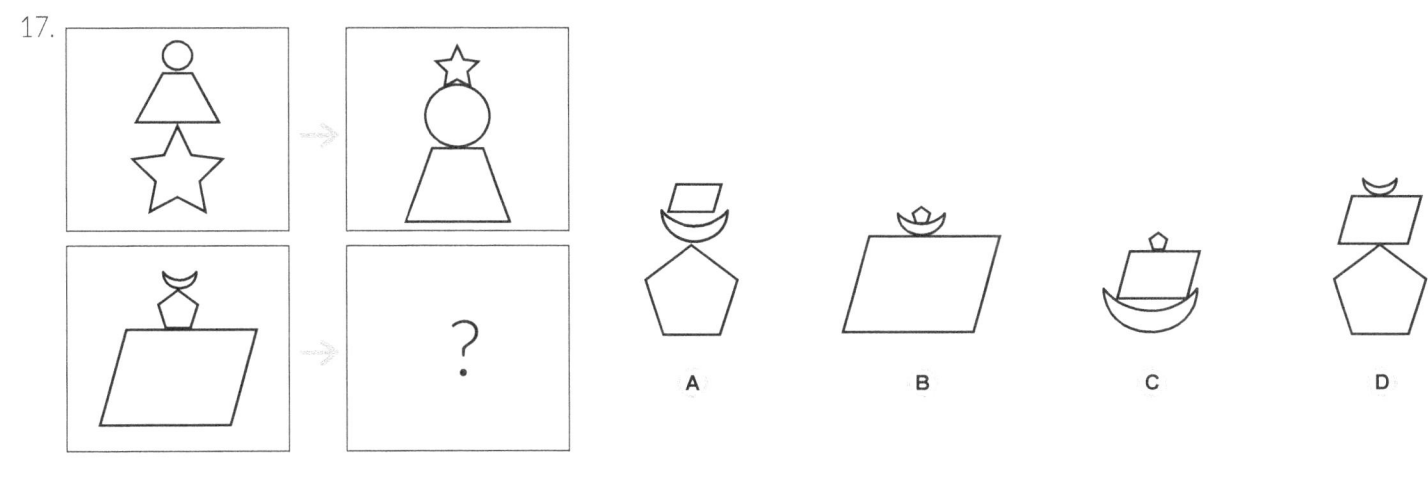

18.

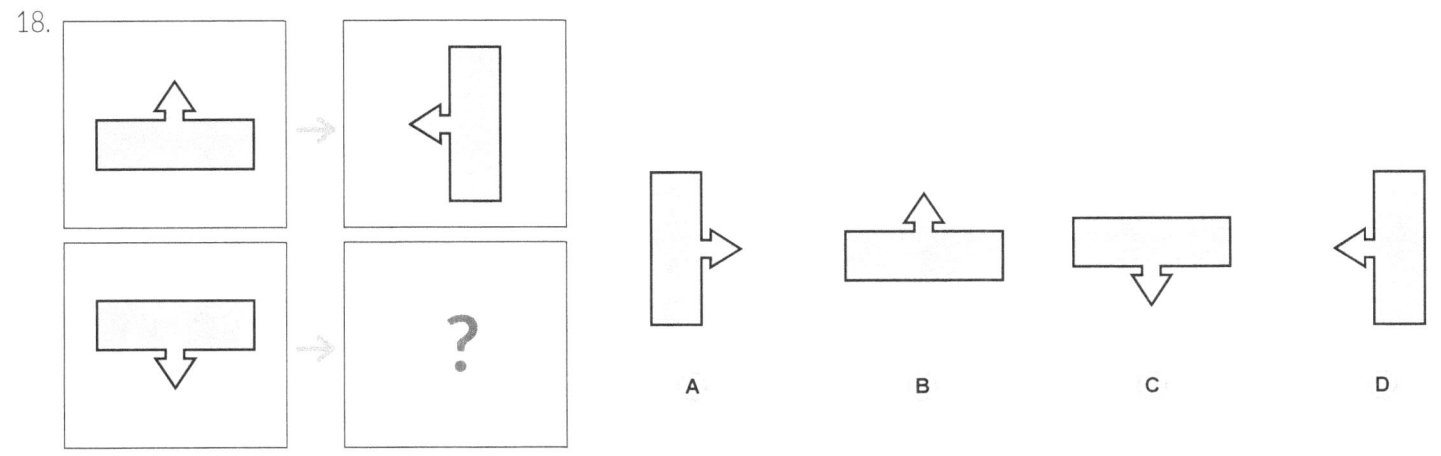

63

FIGURE CLASSIFICATION
Directions: The top row shows three pictures that are alike in some way. Look at the bottom row. Which bottom picture goes best with the top pictures?

1.

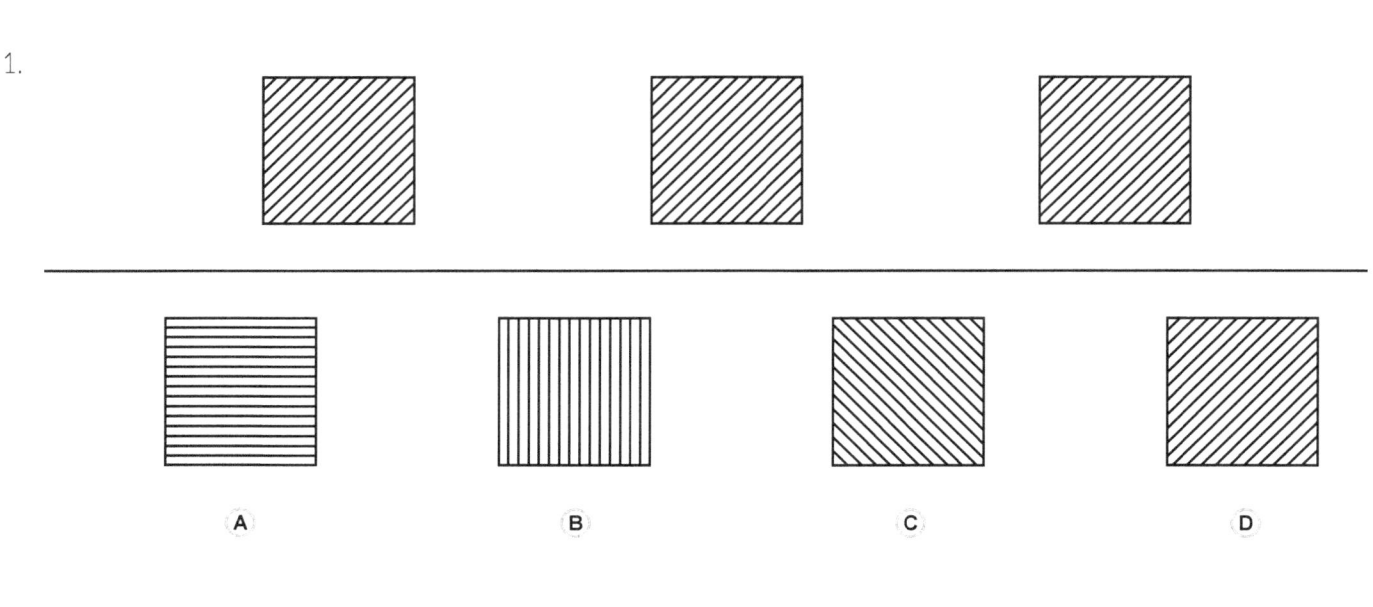

2.

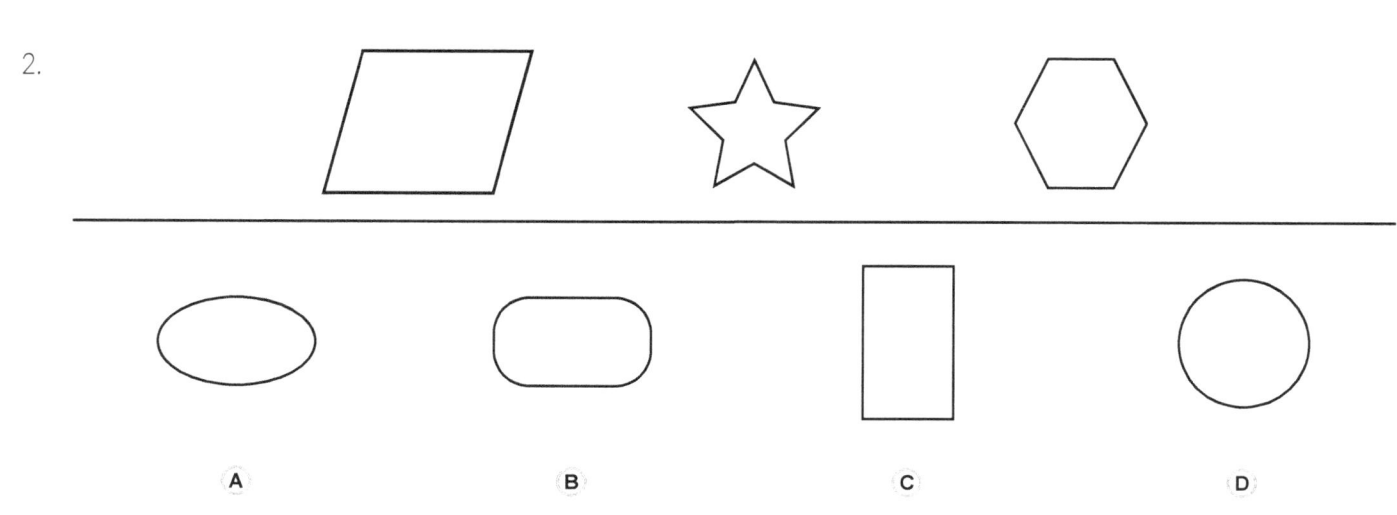

3.

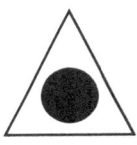 | 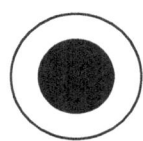 | 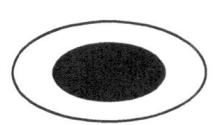 |

A   B   C   D

4.

      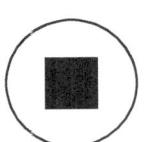

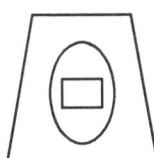   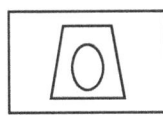   

A   B   C   D

5.

      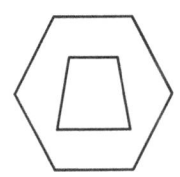   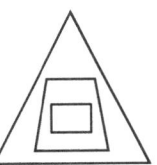

A   B   C   D

6.

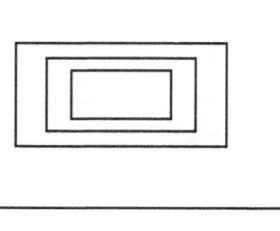  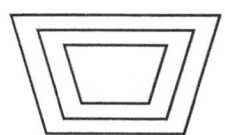

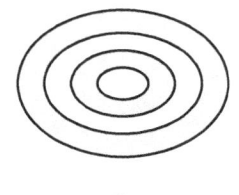 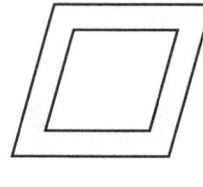  

(A)   (B)   (C)   (D)

7.

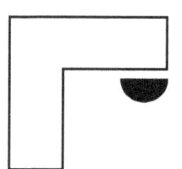 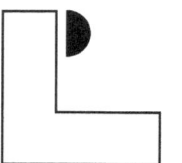 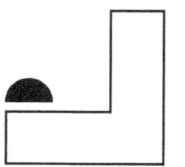

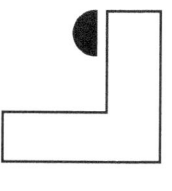 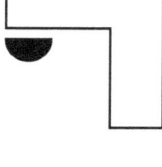 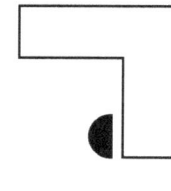 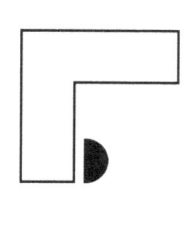

A   B   C   D

8.

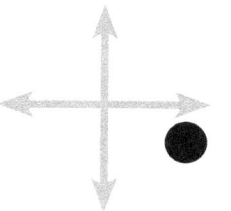 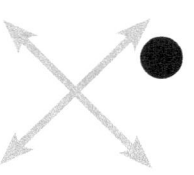 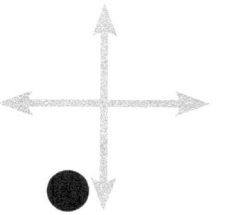

A   B   C   D

9.

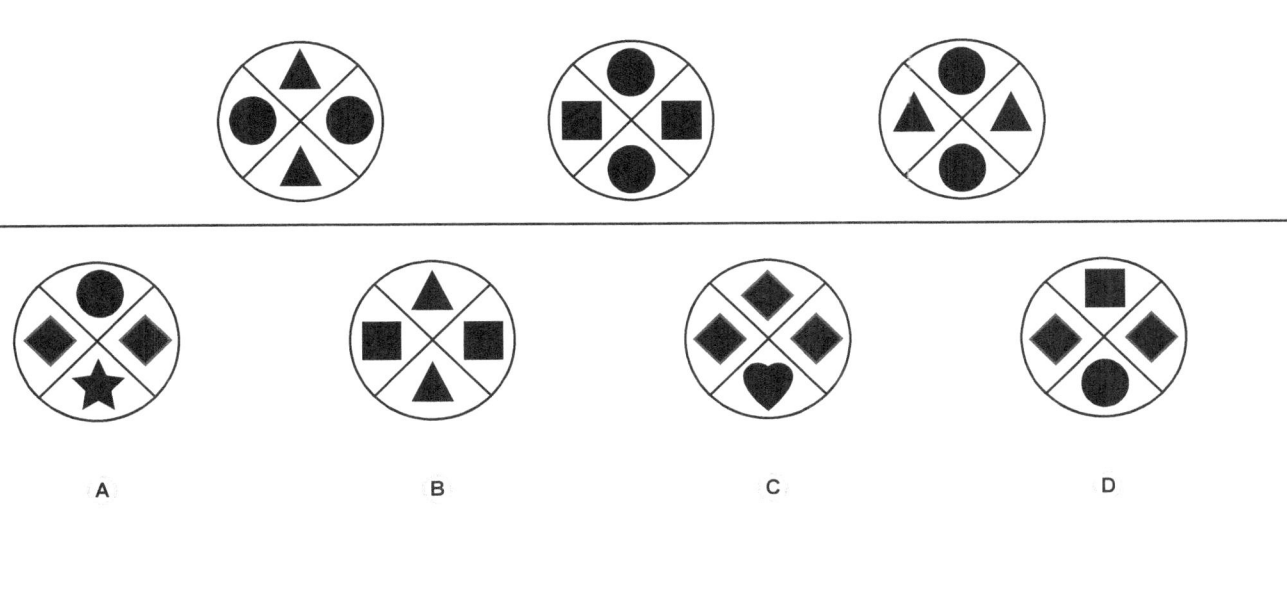

A   B   C   D

10.

A   B   C   D

11.

A   B   C   D

12.

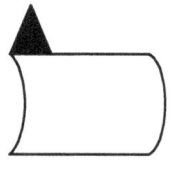

A

B

C

D

13.

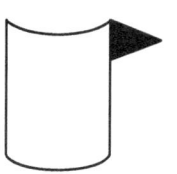

A

B

C

D

14.

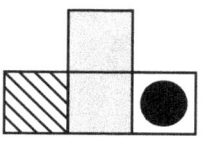

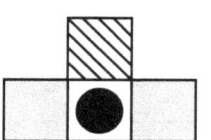

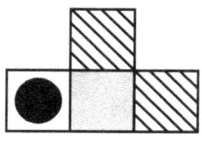 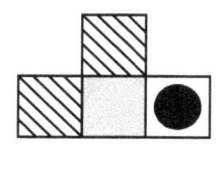 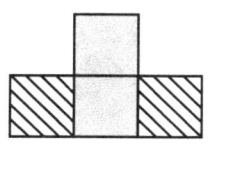

A

B

C

D

15.

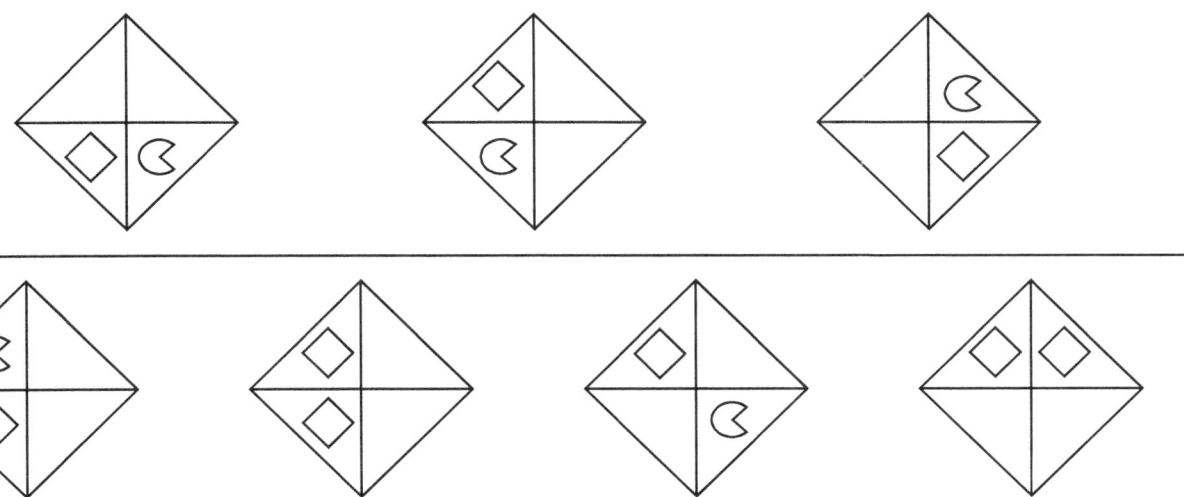

A   B   C   D

16.

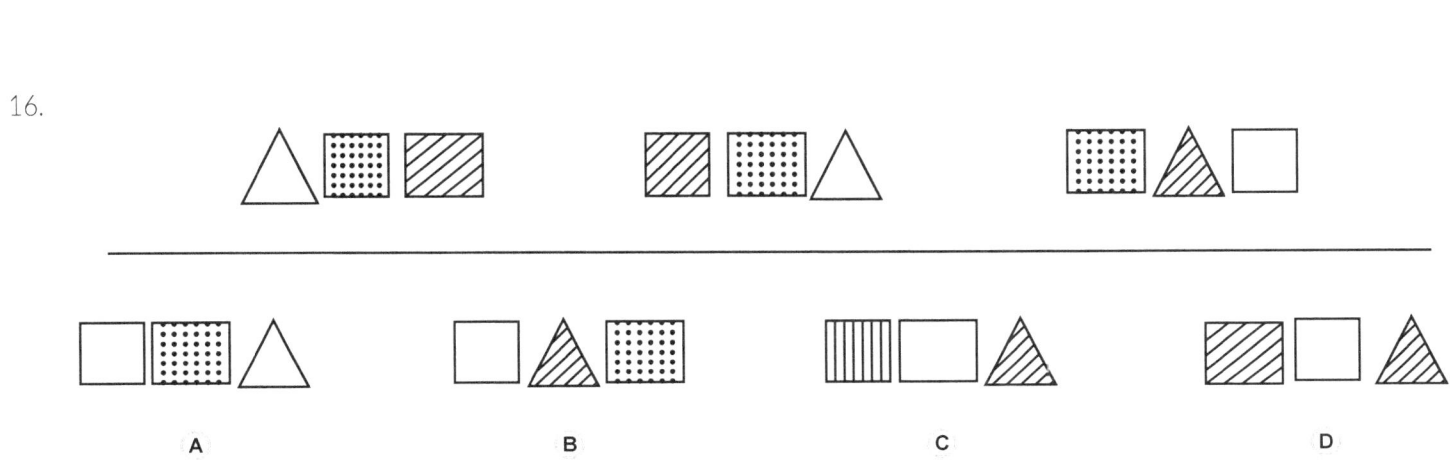

A   B   C   D

17.

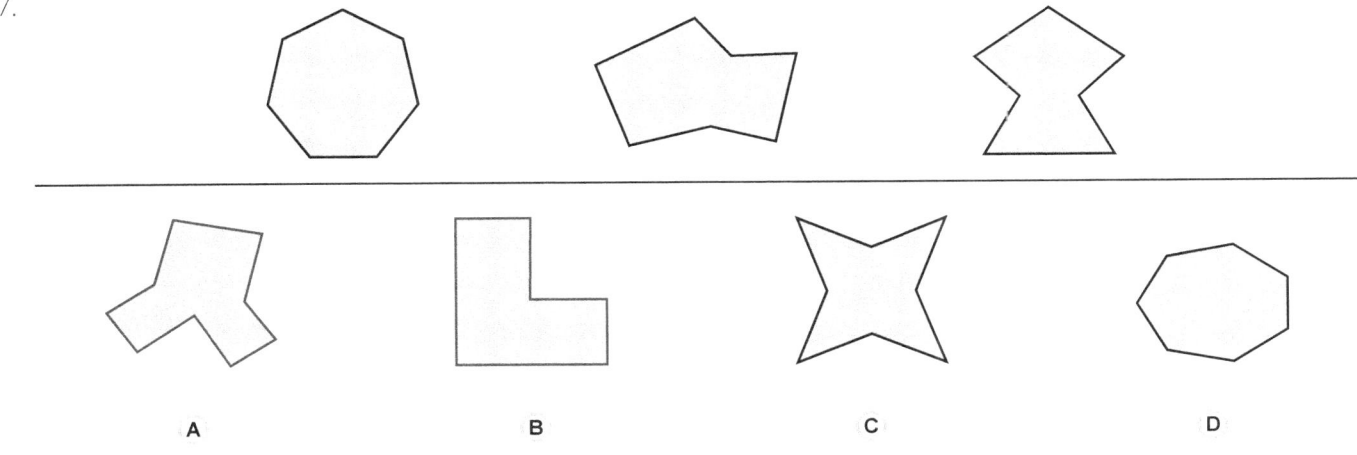

A   B   C   D

PAPER FOLDING

Which picture in the bottom row shows how the paper would look after it's unfolded?

1.

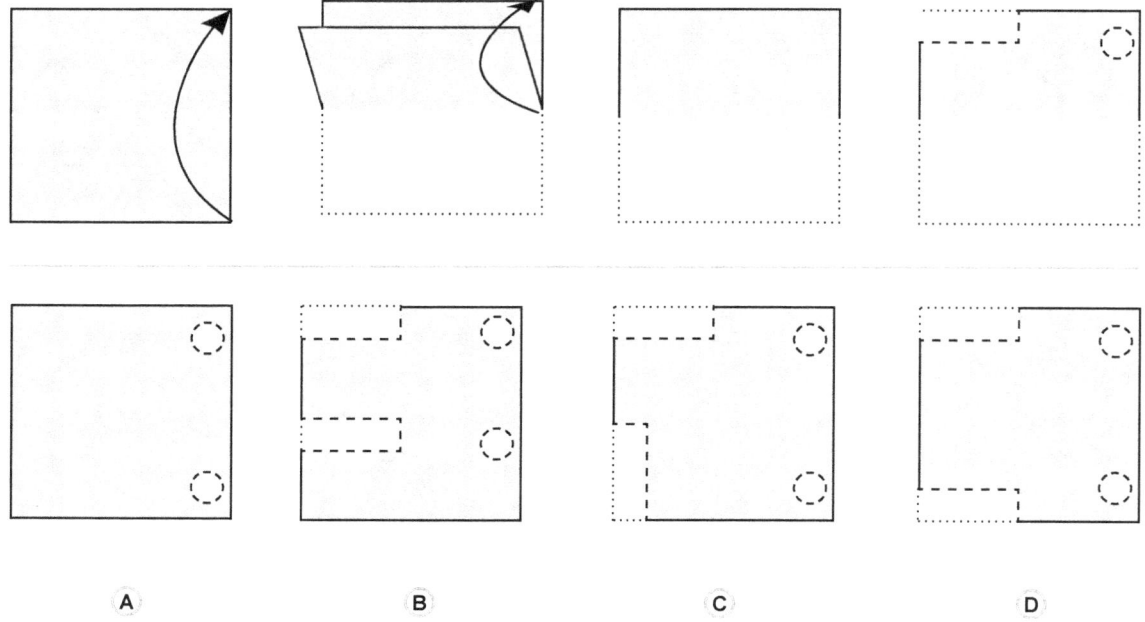

2.

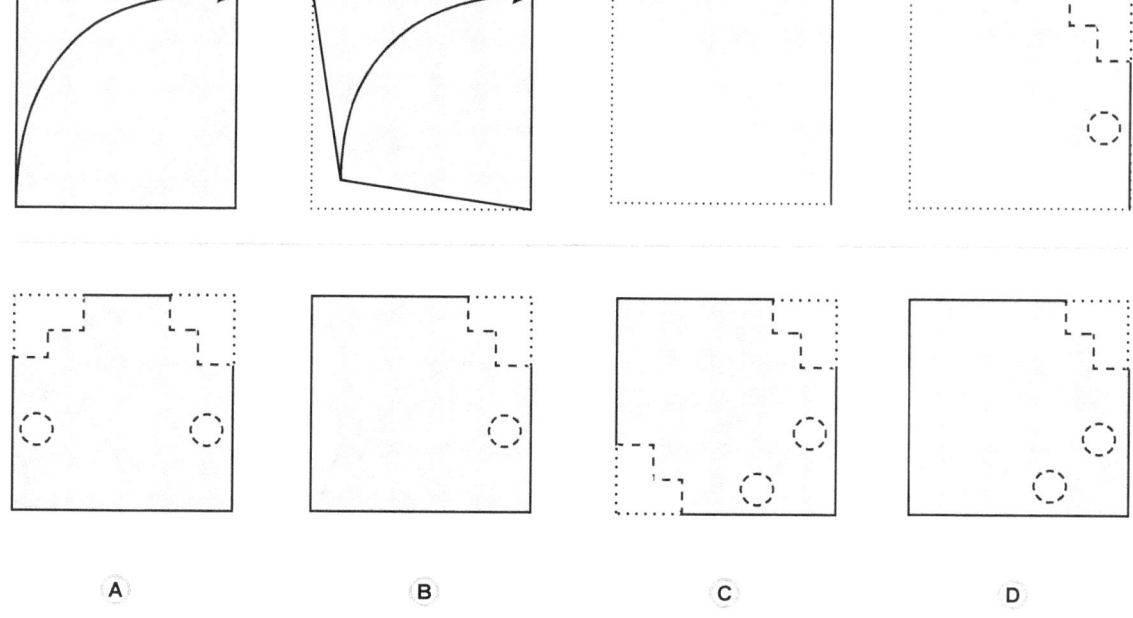

3.

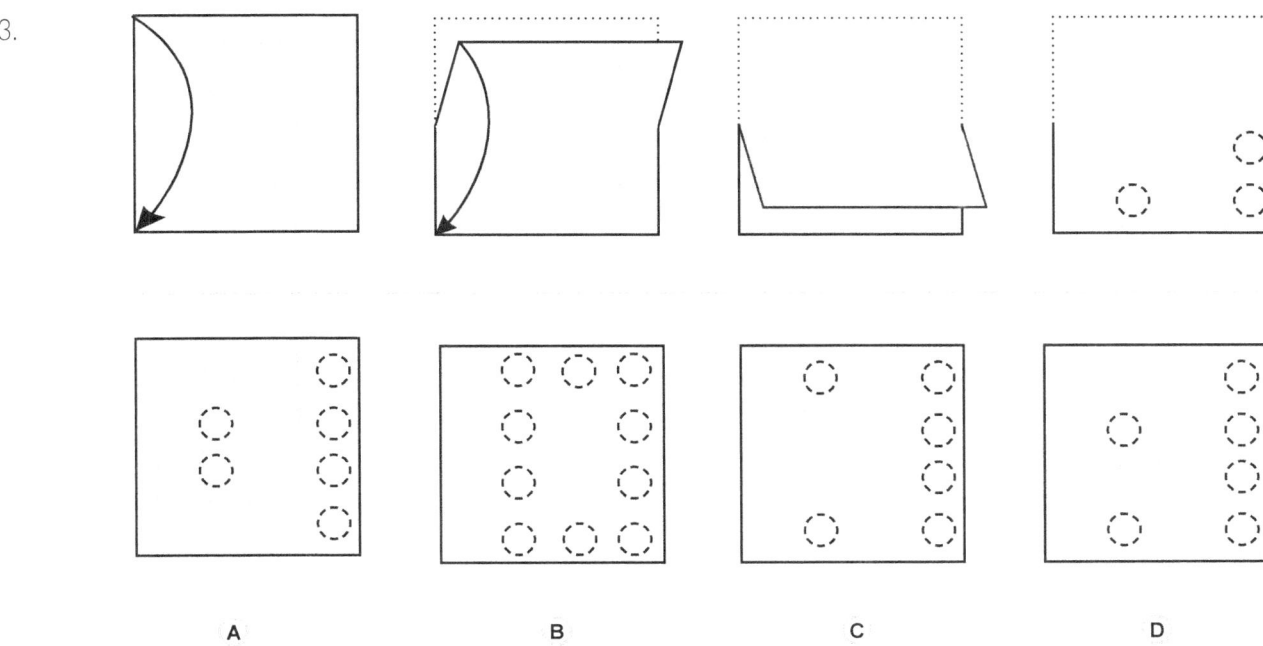

| A | B | C | D |

4.

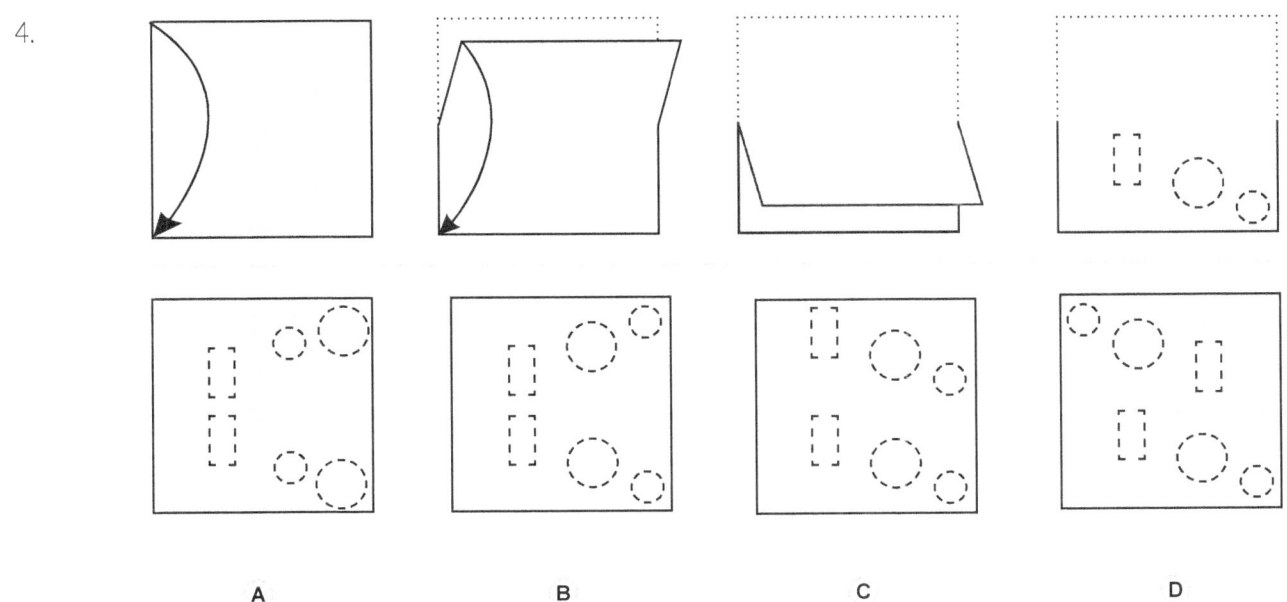

| A | B | C | D |

5.

A   B   C   D

6.

A   B   C   D

7.

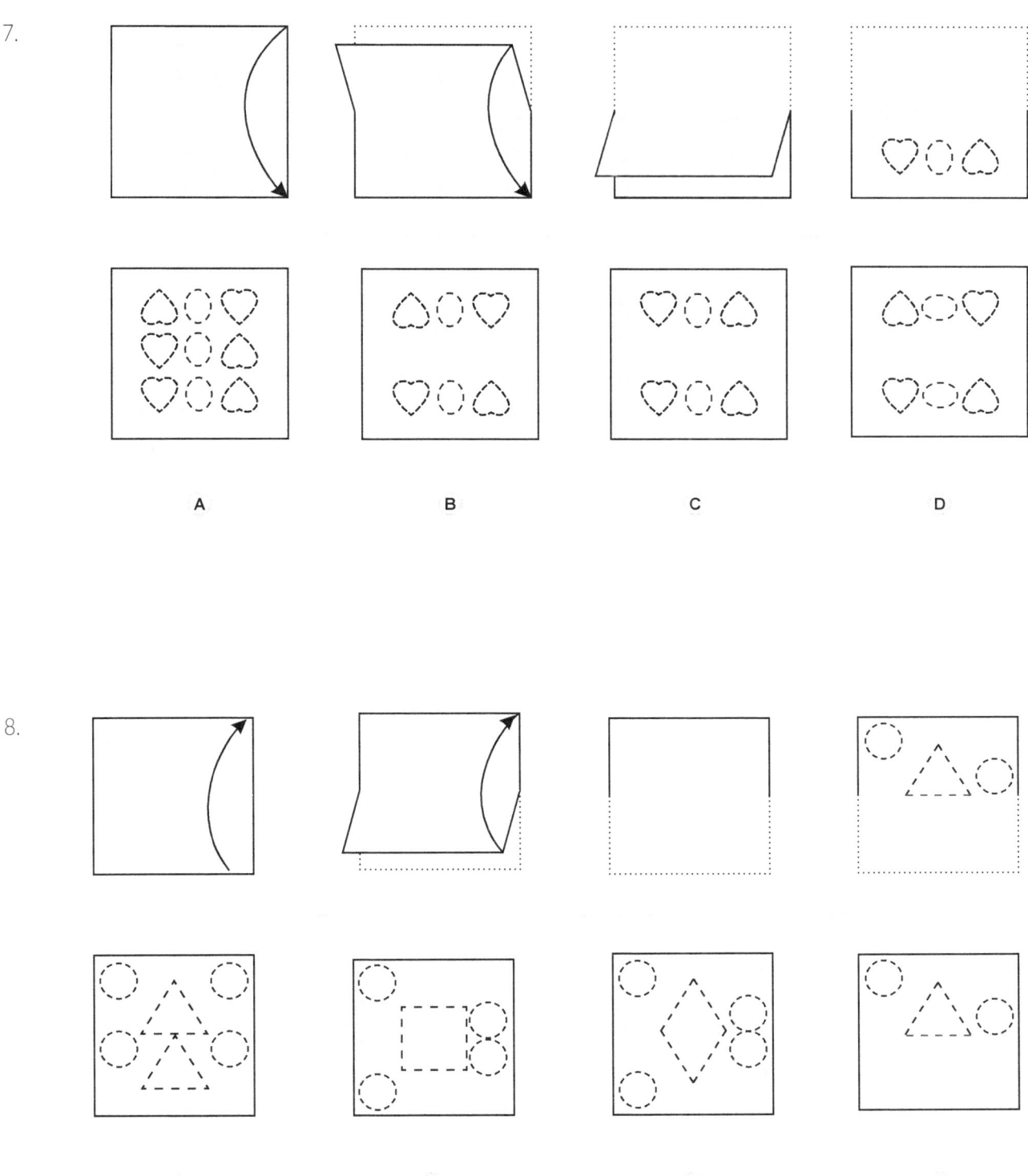

A   B   C   D

8.

A   B   C   D

9.

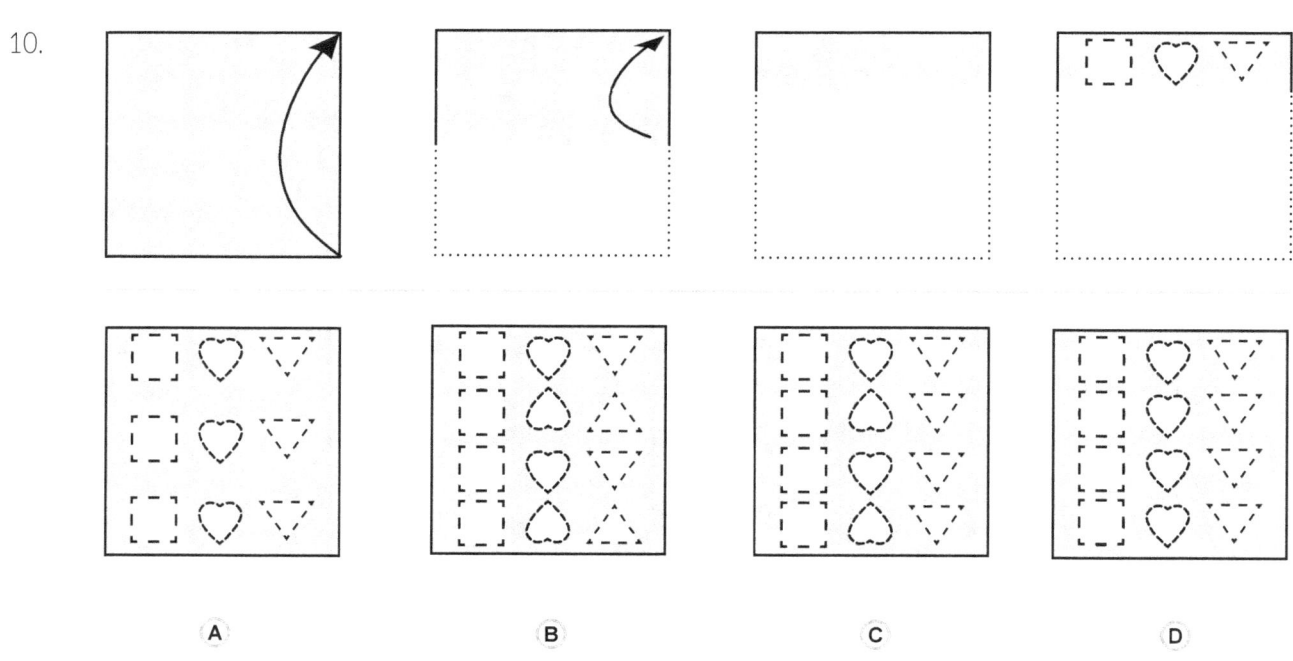

A   B   C   D

10.

A   B   C   D

74

11.

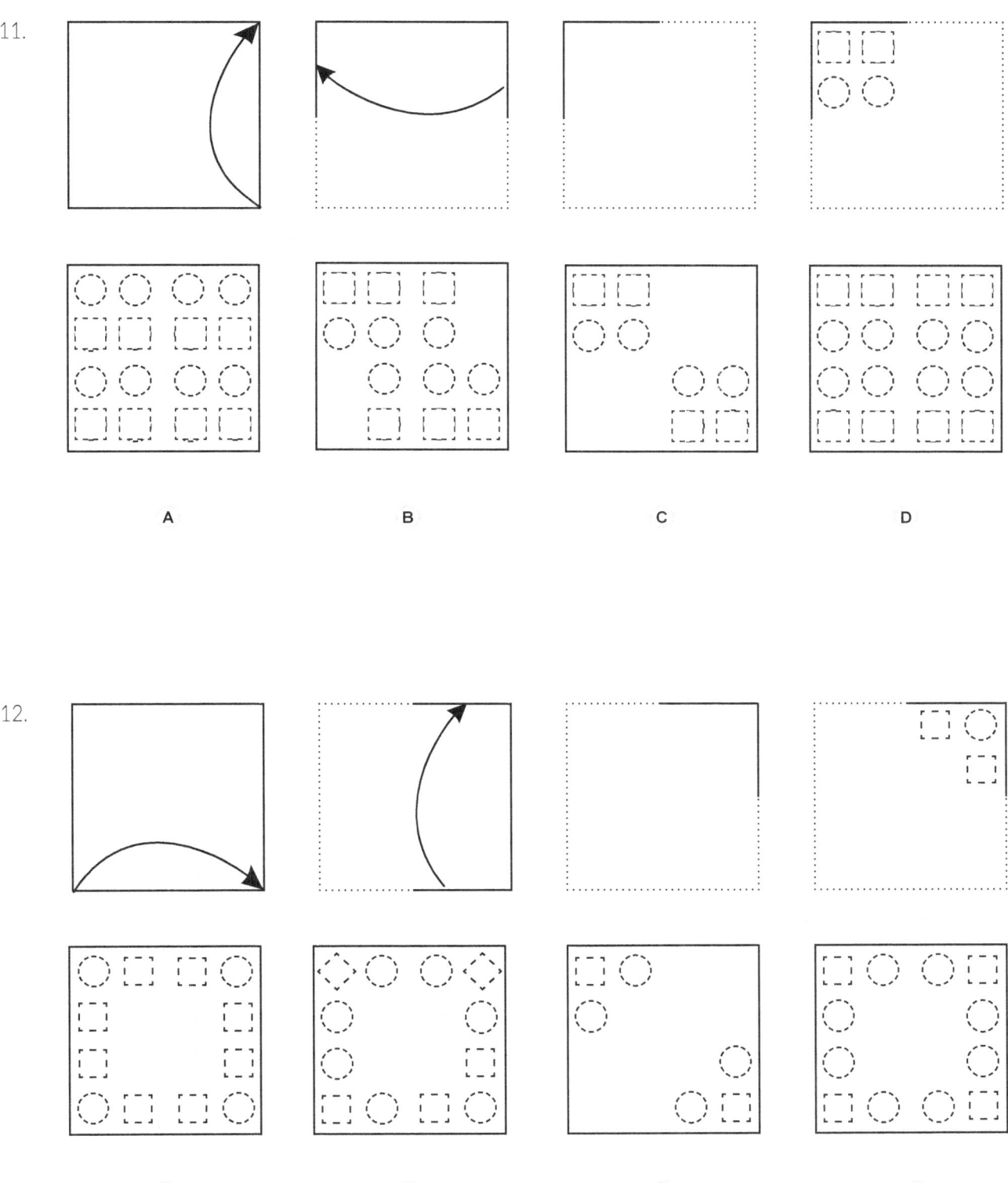

A   B   C   D

12.

A   B   C   D

13.

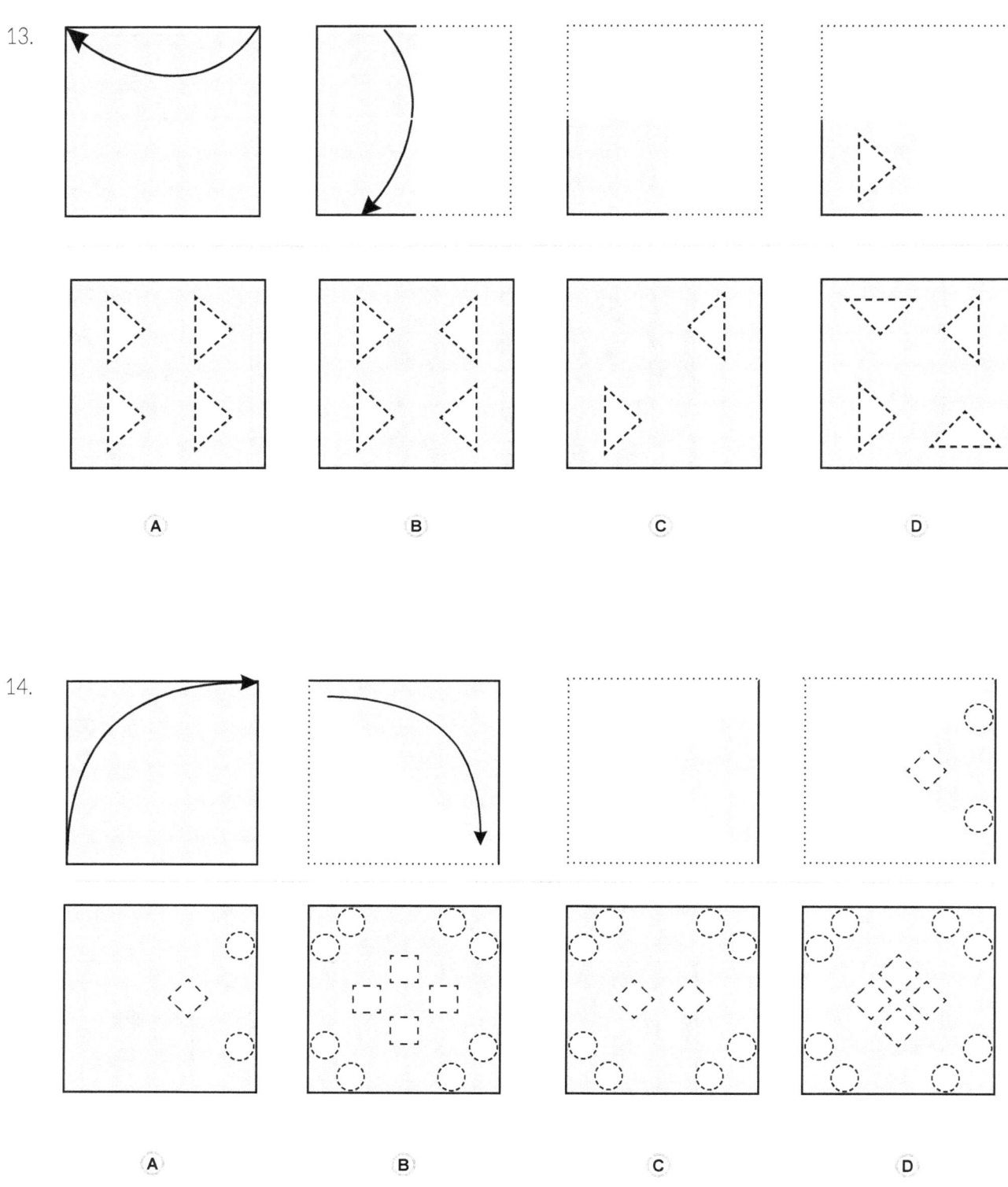

| A | B | C | D |

14.

- End of Practice Test 3 -

ANSWER KEYS

ANSWER KEY FOR PRACTICE TEST 1 (WORKBOOK FORMAT)

Figure Analogies, Practice Test 1

-1. C. A smaller, white version of the original gray shape appears in the middle of the original shape.

-2. B. The original shape is divided in half. The bottom half is black.

-3. C. The smaller center shape moves to the top of the larger white shape.

-4. D. The shape rotates 180 degrees.

-5. D. The shape flips/becomes a mirror image of the original. Or, the shape rotates 90 degrees clockwise.

-6. A. The shape gets bigger and is black.

-7. B. The smaller shape moves to the right side of the line.

-8. C. The smaller, inner shape gets bigger and becomes the outer shape. The larger, outer shape gets smaller and becomes the inner shape.

-9. D. A shape with one more side appears in the second box. On top, there is a triangle (3 sides), followed by a rectangle (4 sides). On bottom, there is a pentagon (5 sides), followed by a hexagon (6 sides).

-10. A. The shapes switch colors (black and gray).

-11. D. The shape group rotates 90 degrees clockwise.

-12. B. One more shape of the same color is added (triangles on top, thin ovals on the bottom).

-13. B. The squares switch colors (black and white).

-14. B. The smaller, inner shape gets bigger and becomes the outer shape. The larger, outer shape gets smaller and becomes the inner shape. Then, the shapes switch colors (white and black).

-15. C. A gray triangle becomes a white circle and vice versa. The bottom shape changes color (white to gray on top & gray to white on bottom).

-16. D. The larger outer shape becomes the smallest inner shape. The smallest inner shape becomes the larger outer shape.

-17. A. The figure "flips" down to become a mirror image.

-18. C. The top shape becomes the middle shape and gets bigger. The middle shape becomes the bottom shape and gets bigger. The bottom shape becomes the top shape and gets smaller.

Figure Classification, Practice Test 1

-1. C. The shapes are trapezoids.

-2. B. The shapes have horizontal lines.

-3. A. There is only one arrow. It points to either the right or left.

-4. D. The shapes are ovals divided in half.

-5. D. The shapes are divided in half.

-6. B. The design follows the pattern: white, dotted, white.

-7. B. The left and right sections of the circle have the same smaller shapes.

-8. D. The vertically-aligned group of 3 shapes has a large shape in the middle and two of the same smaller shape on the top and bottom.

-9. D. There are 2 triangles pointing up and 1 point down.

-10. C. There is 1 of each: black circle, black square, white circle, white square.

-11. B. Half of the circle is white and half is black.

-12. C. Four shapes are in the group.

-13. A. The same small, middle shape (a "pac-man") is in the middle of the shape group.

-14. D. There are 3 gray squares. Two gray squares are next to each other and the other one touches one corner of the group of 2.

-15. D. The shapes have 8 sides.

-16. A. The circles have 4 lines inside.

-17. B. There are 2 shapes of the same type & design inside on the left and right. There is 1 shape of another type & color in the middle.

-18. D. As the shape group rotates, the circle remains at the same position on the heart.

Paper Folding, Practice Test 1

-1. C	-2. D	-3. D	-4. B
-5. B	-6. B	-7. A	-8. C
-9. C	-10. A	-11. D	-12. C
-13. B	-14. D	-15. B	-16. D
-17. B			

ANSWER KEY FOR PRACTICE TEST 2

Figure Analogies, Practice Test 2

-1. C. The shape changes from gray to filled with diagonal lines going from lower left to upper right.

-2. C. A smaller, white version of the original black shape appears in the middle of the original shape.

-3. D. The shape is divided in half vertically.

-4. B. The shapes switch position (left and right) and color (gray and white).

-5. A. The same shape appears in the second box.

-6. D. The shape rotates 90 degrees clockwise and changes from black to gray.

-7. C. Circles become X's. X's become circles.

-8. D. The colors switch.

-9. A. The smaller, inner shape gets bigger and becomes the outer shape. The larger, outer shape gets smaller and becomes the inner shape. Then, the colors switch.

-10. C. The top and middle shapes switch positions.

-11. C. The design inside the larger outer shape and the two smaller inner shapes switch. Also, the smaller shapes change from aligning vertically to aligning horizontally.

-12. B. A black pentagon becomes a gray heart and vice versa. The bottom shape changes color (gray to black on top & black to gray on bottom).

-13. C. In the divided square, the objects in the top left and the bottom right switch positions (the triangle & star on top and the "O" and the "A" on bottom).

-14. D. In the 2 groups of hearts (the top group and the bottom group), 1 heart is added on top and 1 heart is taken away on the bottom.

-15. C. The shapes that remain are those that are gray in the first box. Then, they switch to white.

-16. D. The number of arrow points equals the number of shape sides. A shape with the same number of sides appears in the second box.

-17. D. The group of squares rotates 90 degrees clockwise. Then, the colors switch.

Figure Classification, Practice Test 2

-1. D. The shapes are divided into equal parts (halves or quarters).

-2. C. In the shape group, there is 1 star in the center of the gray square.

-3. D. Each shape group has: 1 large square, 1 (and only 1) circle, 1 (and only 1) hexagon.

-4. A. There are 2 shapes of the same type & design inside on the left and right. There is 1 shape of another type & color in the middle.

-5. D. The figures are 2-pointed arrows.

Figure Classification, Practice Test 2, continued

-6. D. There is 1 (and only 1) gray square in each group.

-7. C. Each shape group has 2 of the same shape next to each other.

-8. B. The thin rectangle is next to the base of the arrow's pointed part.

-9. D. The shape group consists of 1 large center shape and 2 smaller versions of that same shape on the right and left.

-10. A. There are 2 dotted bars and 1 gray bar.

-11. A. There are 3 circles filled with dots.

-12. B. The large shape is the opposite color of the small shapes.

-13. D. Half the shape is gray, and half is white.

-14. C. The arrows point up.

-15. A. As the shape group rotates, the circle stays at the same spot on the arrow point.

(Note that choice B and D are not correct. You can find the same arrows in the top row, but the circle is not at the same spot. Choice C has the circle in the wrong spot as well.)

Paper Folding, Practice Test 2

-1. A

-2. C

-3. D

-4. B

-5. C

-6. C

-7. C

-8. D

-9. B

-10. A

-11. A

-12. D

-13. C

-14. B

-15. A

-16. C

ANSWER KEY FOR PRACTICE TEST 3

Figure Analogies, Practice Test 3

-1. B. The arrow flips (becomes a mirror image) and becomes black.

-2. C. The shapes switch colors (white & gray).

-3. C. The shapes switch colors (gray & black).

-4. A. The figures (plus sign & O's on top and M's and L's on bottom) switch positions.

-5. C. The colors switch (gray & white).

-6. B. The top and bottom shapes rotate 180 degrees. (Also, the same shape group appears in the top left box & bottom right box and the top right box & bottom left box).

-7. D. The signs & shapes reverse order.

-8. A. The black background shape is removed. Then, the gray shape rotates 180 degrees.

-9. D. The 2 shapes flip (become a mirror image of the original), become white, and move closer.

-10. A. The shape divides horizontally. Then, the shape rotates 180 degrees. Finally, the bottom part is the same color as the original shape, but the top part is the opposite color.

-11. B. The shapes align vertically. The smaller and larger shapes switch positions, sizes, and colors.

-12. D. The shapes align vertically and switch designs (gray & black in top boxes and dotted & gray in bottom boxes).

-13. D. The circles and squares are divided in half. The circle halves switch color. The square halves switch color.

-14. C. The squares switch their inside design like this: black becomes gray, gray becomes black, black lines become white, and white becomes black lines. Or, you could say that squares 1 & 2 switch and squares 3 & 4 switch.

-15. D. The original shape rotates 180 degrees and another one just like it is added.

-16. C. The circles switch color from black to gray and from gray to black. The shape in the lower left corner changes from a star to square, changes its color, and moves to the top right corner.

-17. A. The top shape becomes the middle shape and gets bigger. The middle shape becomes the bottom shape and gets bigger. The bottom shape becomes the top shape and gets smaller.

-18. A. The shape rotates 90 degrees counterclockwise.

Figure Classification, Practice Test 3

-1. D. The diagonal lines go from the lower left to the upper right.

-2. C. The shapes have angled corners. (Choice A and D are circles and have no corners. Choice B has rounded corners.)

-3. D. Three shapes point up, and 1 shape points down.

-4. A. The white shape and black shape are different types of shapes.
-5. B. Each shape group has 3 shapes: a trapezoid, rectangle, and oval.
-6. C. There are 3 shapes in each group. The first is gray. The second is white. The third is gray.
-7. C. As the shape group rotates, the black half circle remains at the same spot on the white "L" shape.
-8. C. As the shape group rotates, the black circle remains at the same location on the arrow group.
-9. D. On the bottom, the top shape has been rotated 90 degrees clockwise.
-10. D. The shapes are divided into 3 equal parts.
-11. B. In the divided circle, the top & bottom shapes are the same, and the left and right shapes are the same.
-12. C. The hearts form 3-in-a-row (tic-tac-toe).
-13. A. As the shape group rotates, the black triangle remains at the same location on the white shape.
-14. A. In the shape group, there are 2 gray squares, 1 square filled with diagonal lines, and 1 white square with a black circle inside.
-15. A. In the divided diamond, the small white diamond and the small white "pac-man" are next to each other.
-16. B. In each group is: 1 white shape, 1 shape with diagonal lines, and 1 shape with dotted lines.
-17. D. The shapes have 7 sides.

Paper Folding, Practice Test 3

-1. D	-2. C	-3. C	-4. B	-5. A	-6. A	-7. B
-8. C	-9. B	-10. B	-11. D	-12. A	-13. B	-14. D

Need more practice?

- Help your child **ace the test**!

- Check out **Savant Test Prep**™ books on Amazon®.